MARRYING OFF MOTHER

AND OTHER STORIES

Gerald Durrell was one of Britain's best loved authors and pioneering naturalists. His books, such as the bestselling *My Family and Other Animals* which celebrated its 50th anniversary in 2006, continue to entertain generations of children and adults alike.

The Durrell Wildlife Conservation Trust
is an international conservation charity
with headquarters in Jersey, UK.

'A renegade who was right . . .
He was truly a man before his time'

SIR DAVID ATTENBOROUGH

Gerald Durrell

MARRYING OFF MOTHER

AND OTHER STORIES

BRIDE – a woman with a fine prospect of happiness
behind her

AMBROSE BIERCE, *The Devil's Dictionary*

PAN BOOKS

First published 1991 by HarperCollins

This edition published 2016 by Pan Books
an imprint of Pan Macmillan
20 New Wharf Road, London N1 9RR
Associated companies throughout the world
www.panmacmillan.com

ISBN 978-1-5098-2934-7

A CIP catalogue record for this book is available from the British Library.

Printed and bound by CPI Group (UK) Ltd, Croydon, CR0 4YY

Visit **www.panmacmillan.com** to read more about all our books
and to buy them. You will also find features, author interviews and
news of any author events, and you can sign up for e-newsletters
so that you're always first to hear about our new releases.

This book is for
Teeny and Hal
T.B.M.I.L. *and* T.B.F.I.L.
from Gerry
T.B.S.I.L.I.T.W.
With all my love

Contents

A Word in Advance

All of these stories are true or, to be strictly accurate, some are true, some have a kernel of truth and a shell of embroidery. Some were my own experiences, others were told to me and I appropriated them for my own purposes, which bears out the saying: 'Never talk to an author if you don't want to appear in print'.

Which of these stories is true and which is semi-true I have, of course, not the slightest intention of telling you, but I hope this will not detract from your enjoyment of them.

Gerald Durrell

Esmeralda

Of all the many regions in La Belle France, there is one whose very name adds a lustrous glitter to the eye of a gourmet, a flush of anticipation to his cheeks, that drenches his taste buds with anticipatory saliva, and that is the euphonious name of Périgord. Here the chestnuts and walnuts are of prodigious size, here the wild strawberries are as heavily scented as a courtesan's boudoir. Here the apples, the pears and the plums have sublime juices captured in their skins, here the flesh of the chicken, duckling and pigeon is firm and white, here the butter is as yellow as sunshine and the cream on top of the churns is thick enough to balance a full glass of wine upon. As well as all these riches, Périgord has one supreme prize that lurks beneath the loamy soil of her oak woods, the truffle, the troglodyte fungus that lives beneath the surface of the forest floor, black as a witch's cat, delicious as all the perfumes of Arabia.

In this delectable part of the world I had found a small and charming village and had put up at the tiny local hostelry called Les Trois Pigeons. Here, mine host, Jean Pettione, was a jovial fellow whose face had been turned by wine to the russet colour of a pippin. At this period in autumn the woods were in their prime, a rich tapestry of colours from gold to bronze. Wishing to enjoy them, I got M. Pettione to do me a picnic lunch and drove into the countryside. I parked the car and walked off into the forest to enjoy the panoply of colours and the strange and magical shapes of the toadstools that grow everywhere. Presently, I sat down on the sturdy carcase of an elderly oak to enjoy my lunch and just as

I had finished there was a rustling in the dead ginger-coloured bracken and an enormous pig appeared. She was as surprised to see me as I was to see her. We gazed at each other with interest.

She weighed, I guessed, somewhere in the neighbourhood of sixteen stone. She was sleekly pink with a peach bloom of white hair and a few decorative black spots placed by Nature as carefully and seductively as the dark patches that ladies in the 1600s used to adorn themselves with. She had small golden eyes full of wisdom and mischief, her ears drooped down each side of her face like a nun's habit and then there, jutting out proudly, was her snout, delicately wrinkled, the end of it looking like one of those splendid Victorian instruments you use for clearing blocked drains. Her hooves were elegant and polished, and her tail a wonderful wind-up pink question mark, propelling her through life. She had about her an aura not, as one would assume, of pig but a delicate fragrant scent that conjured up spring meadows ablaze with flowers. I had never smelt a pig like her. I searched my mind as to where I had last encountered this magical romantic perfume and at last I remembered. I had got into the lift in the hotel I was staying at and the delicious lady who was travelling downwards with me also had wafted this delectable aroma to me as the pig was now doing. I had asked the lady in the lift if she would mind vouchsafing to me the name of her exquisite perfume, and she told me it was called Joy.

Now, I have had many strange experiences in life, but until then I had never been privileged to meet, in an oak forest in Périgord, a large and amiable pig wearing this particular and expensive scent. She moved slowly up to me, placed her chin on my knee and uttered a prolonged and rather alarming grunt, the sort of noise a Harley Street specialist makes when he is about to tell you the disease you are suffering from will be fatal. She sighed deeply and then commenced to chomp her jaws together. The sound was like the noise made by an extraordinarily agile group of Spanish dancers with an abundance of castanets. She sighed again. It was obvious the lady wanted something. She nosed at my bag, uttering small squeals of delight when I opened it to see what was exciting her. All I could see was the remains of the cheese I had been eating. I took it out, circumnavigated her efforts to seize the whole thing and cut her off a slice. It slid into her mouth and there, to my astonishment, she let it lie, enjoying the fragrance as a wine expert will let a wine lie along his tongue, breathing its perfume, tasting its body. Then slowly and carefully she started to eat it, uttering tiny mumbling noises of satisfaction. I noticed that she wore around her portly neck, as a dowager would wear a waterfall of pearls, a very elegant collar of gold chain and dangling from it was a length of chain which had been snapped in half. So elegant was she that it was obvious that my new found friend was a pig that someone valued, and had lost. She took some more cheese, uttering little grunts of thanks and pleasure, letting each fragment lie for a moment on her tongue like a true connoisseur. I saved one piece of cheese as a lure and with it got her out of the wood and alongside my station-wagon. She was obviously quite used to this form of transport and she climbed into the back and settled herself down comfortably, staring around in regal fashion, her mouth full of cheese. As I drove back towards the village which I felt sure was her home, the pig rested her chin on my shoulder and went to sleep. I decided that the mixture of the scent of Joy with that of ripe Roquefort was not a combination guaranteed to attract a member of the opposite sex. I stopped at Les Trois Pigeons, removed the redolent pig's head from my shoulder, gave her the last bit of cheese and went inside in search of the redoubtable Jean. He was busily polishing glasses with great precision, breathing heartily on each one to get the required shine.

'Jean,' I said, 'I have a problem.'

'A problem, monsieur, what problem?' he asked.

'I have acquired a pig,' I said.

'Monsieur has purchased a pig?' he asked in astonishment.

'No, I did not purchase it, I acquired it. I was sitting in the forest eating my lunch when this pig suddenly appeared and offered to share my food with me. I believe it to be an unusual pig since it not only has a passion for Roquefort cheese, but it was wearing a gold chain collar and smelled strongly of perfume.'

The glass he was polishing slipped through his fingers and fell to the floor, shattering into a multitude of fragments.

'Mon Dieu!' he said, his eyes wide. 'You have Esmeralda!'

'There was no name on the collar,' I said, 'but there can't be many pigs answering to that description trotting about, so I suppose she must be Esmeralda. Who does she belong to?'

He came round the counter, glass scrunching under his feet, taking off his apron.

'She belongs to Monsieur Clot,' he said. 'Mon Dieu! He will go mad if he has lost her. Where is she?'

'In my car,' I replied, 'finishing off a slice of the Roquefort.'

We went out to the station-wagon and saw that Esmeralda, finding that a cruel fate was denying her any more cheese, had philosophically fallen asleep. Her snores made the whole vehicle tremble as if the engine was still running.

'Oh! la la!' said Jean. 'It *is* Esmeralda. Oh, Monsieur Clot will be out of his mind. You must take her back to him *at once*, Monsieur. Monsieur Clot thinks the world of that pig. You must take her back *immediately*.'

'Well, I will be happy to do that,' I said, a trifle testily, 'if you tell me where Monsieur Clot lives. I don't want my life encumbered by a pig.'

'A *pig*!' said Jean, looking at me in horror. 'That is not just a pig, monsieur, it is *Esmeralda*.'

'I don't care what her name is,' I said, crossly, 'at the moment she is in my car, smelling like a Parisian tart that's been on a cheese jag, and the sooner I get rid of her the happier I will be.'

Jean drew himself up and stared at me.

'A tart?' he said. 'You call her a tart? Esmeralda, as everyone knows, is a virgin.'

I began to feel that my mind was becoming unhinged. Was I really standing next to my station-wagon in which slept a highly aromatic pig called Esmeralda and discussing her sex life with the owner of a hotel called the Three Pigeons? I took a deep breath to steady myself.

4

Look,' I said, 'I don't care about Esmeralda's sex life. I don't care if she has been raped by all the boar pigs in Périgord.'

'Oh! Mon Dieu! She hasn't been raped, has she?' croaked Jean, his face going white.

'No, no, no, not to the best of my knowledge. She has not been deflowered or whatever it is you do to a pig. In any case, it would take a particularly lascivious boar and one with no olfactory senses left, to attempt to rape a sow pig smelling like a high class whore on a Saturday night.'

'Please, *please*, monsieur,' said Jean, in agony, 'don't say things like that – particularly in front of Monsieur Clot. He treats her with all the reverence you would accord a saint.'

I was about to say something irreverent about St Gadarene, but checked myself for Jean obviously took the whole thing very seriously.

'Look,' I said, 'if Monsieur Clot has lost Esmeralda he will be worried, won't he?'

'Worried – *worried*? He'll be insane.'

'Well, then, the sooner I get Esmeralda back to him the better. Now, where does he live?'

Having been brought up in Greece where distance was to be measured in cigarettes – of little use to me at the age of ten – I had become fairly adept at extracting directions from local people. One had to approach it with all the dedication of an archaeologist brushing away the dust of ages to reveal an artefact. The chief problem was that people always assumed that you had their intimate knowledge of the surrounding terrain and so it took time and patience. Jean, as a direction giver, surpassed anything I had come across before.

'Monsieur Clot lives in "Les Arbousiers",' he said.

'And where is that?' I asked.

'You know, his land joins on to Monsieur Mermod's.'

'I don't know Monsieur Mermod.'

'Oh, but you must know him, he's our carpenter. He built all the tables and chairs for Les Trois Pigeons. And the bar, and I think he put the shelves up in the larder, but I'm not sure – that might have been Monsieur Devoir. He lives down in the valley by the river.'

'Where does Monsieur Clot live?'

'Well, I just told you, next door to Monsieur Mermod.'

'How does one get to Monsieur Clot's house?'

'Well, you drive through the village . . . ?'

'Which way?'

'That way,' he said, and pointed.

'And then?'

'You turn left at Mademoiselle Hubert's house and . . .'

'I do not know Mademoiselle Hubert or her house. What does it look like?'

'It is brown.'

'All the houses in the village are brown. How can I recognize it?' He thought deeply.

'Ah,' he said at last, 'today is Thursday. So she will be cleaning. So, enfin, she will hang her little red mat out of the bedroom window.'

'Today is Tuesday.'

'Ah, you are right. If it is Tuesday she will be watering her plants.'

'So I turn left at the brown house where the lady is watering her plants. What then?'

'You drive past the war memorial, past Monsieur Pelligot's house and then, when you come to the tree, you turn left.'

'What tree?'

'The tree at the turning where you turn left.'

'The whole of Périgord is filled with trees. The roads are lined with trees. How can I distinguish this tree from the others?'

Jean looked at me in astonishment.

'Because it is the tree against which Monsieur Herolte killed himself,' he said, 'and it is where his widow goes and lays a wreath in his memory on the anniversary of his death. You can tell it by the wreath.'

'When did he die?'

6

'It was in June 1950, sixth or seventh, I can't be sure. But certainly June.'

'We are now in September – will the wreath still be there?'

'Oh, no, they clear it away when it fades.'

'So is there any other way of identifying the tree?'

'It is an oak,' he said.

'The countryside is full of oaks – how will I know this particular one?'

'It has a dent in it.'

'So there I turn left. Where is Monsieur Clot's house?'

'Oh, you can't miss it. It is a long, low, white building, a real old-style farmhouse.'

'So I just look for a white farmhouse.'

'Yes, but you can't see it from the road.'

'Then how will I know when I am there?'

He thought about this carefully.

'There is a little wooden bridge with one plank missing,' he said. 'That is Monsieur Clot's drive.'

At this point, Esmeralda turned over and we were enveloped in a miasma of perfume and cheese. We moved away from the station-wagon.

'Now,' I said. 'Let me see if I have this straight. I go down there and turn left where a lady is watering her plants. I drive past the war memorial and Monsieur Pelligot's house and continue straight until I come to the oak tree with a dent and then I turn left and look for a bridge with a missing plank. Is that right?'

'Monsieur,' said Jean in admiration, 'you could have been *born* in the village.'

I did find my way at last. At Mademoiselle Hubert's house, she was not watering her plants, nor was her little red mat in evidence. She was in fact sitting in the sun, asleep. Reluctantly, I woke her to ascertain the fact that she was indeed Mademoiselle Hubert at whose house I was supposed to turn left. The oak tree did have a dent in it, a considerable one, so I judged that Monsieur Fierolte must have imbibed an inordinate quantity of pastis before plunging his Deux Chevaux into the bark. The bridge when I found it *did* have a plank missing. The countryman's instructions are always accurate even if they may appear somewhat mysterious when they are vouchsafed to you. I drove down the rutted road on one side of which was a green meadow, bespeckled with a small herd of cream-coloured Charolais cattle, and on the other side was a glittering field of sunflowers, their beautiful yellow and black faces all upturned in adoration of the sun. I drove through a small wood and there, in a clearing, stood Monsieur Clot's house, long and low and white as a dove's egg, its roof made from ancient tiles as thick and dark as bars of chocolate, each emblazoned with the insignia of golden lichens. There were two cars parked outside, one a police car and one a doctor's, and so I slid the station-wagon alongside them. The moment I switched off the engine, rising above Esmeralda's snores I could hear a strange cacophony from the house – shouts, bellows, screams, weepings and wailings and the general gnashing of teeth. I assumed – quite rightly as it turned out – that Esmeralda's disappearance had not gone unnoticed. I went to the front door – which was ajar – and, seizing the Freudian brass knocker representing a hand clasping a ball, I banged loudly. The uproar inside the house continued unabated. I banged again and still no one came. Taking a firm grip on the knocker, I beat the door so ferociously that I feared it might come off its hinges. For a brief moment the bedlam in the house ceased and presently the front door was flung open by one of the most beautiful young women I had ever seen. Her long hair was in disarray, but this only added to its charm, for it was the rich sunset hue that every autumn leaf endeavours to achieve and seldom does. Her skin had been touched and lit by the sun so it had the quality of peach-coloured silk. Her eyes were enormous, a wonderful mixture of green and gold under dark brows like the wings of an albatross. Her pink mouth was of the shape and texture that makes even the most faithful of husbands falter. Tears the size of twenty-two-carat diamonds were flooding from her magnificent eyes and pouring down her cheeks.

'Monsieur?' she questioned, wiping her cheeks with the back of her hand to clear them of the shimmering tears.

'Bonjour, mademoiselle,' I said. 'Could I see Monsieur Clot if you please?'

'Monsieur Clot will see no one,' she said, gulping, and the tears renewed their flow. 'Monsieur Clot is indisposed. He can see no one.'

At that moment, a very large, paunchy gendarme appeared from the back room, where the uproar had now renewed itself. His eyes were as dark as blackcurrants, his nose resplendent, a rich wine red, covered with a patchwork of blue veins, and over his pouting mouth lay an enormous black moustache like the skin of a dead mole. He gave me an all-embracing glance in which suspicion and malevolence were nicely blended. Then he turned to the beautiful lady.

'Madame Clot,' he said, in a rich syrupy voice, 'I must leave now, but rest assured, madame, that I will make the utmost endeavours to unmask the fiends who have perpetrated this outrage, the ghastly assassins who have dared to bring a tear to your beautiful eyes. I will move heaven and earth to bring these brigands to justice.'

He gazed at her like a starving schoolboy regarding a cream-filled doughnut.

'You are too kind, inspector,' she said, flushing.

'For you, nothing is too much trouble – nothing,' he said and, seizing her hand, he pressed her fingertips into his moustache, rather as, in times gone by, a man would help a lady on with her muff. He brushed past me, hurled his bulk into his car and, with an excruciating tangle of gears, drove off in a cloud of dust, a St George in search of a dragon.

'Madame,' I said, 'I see that you are upset, but I feel that it is possible I may be able to help.'

'No one can help – it is hopeless,' she cried, and the tears started to flow again.

'Madame, if I were to mention the name Esmeralda, would this mean anything to you?'

She fell back against the wall, her wonderful eyes staring. 'Esmeralda?' she said, hoarsely.

9

'Esmeralda,' I said.

'Esmeralda?' she repeated.

'Esmeralda,' I nodded.

'You mean *Esmeralda*,' she said faintly.

'Esmeralda the pig,' I said, to make the point clear.

'So you are the fiend in human form – you are the thief who has spirited away our Esmeralda,' she screamed.

'Madame, if you'll just let me explain . . .' I began.

'Thief, robber, bandit,' she wailed, and ran down the passage-way screaming, 'Henri, Henri, Henri, the thief is here demanding a ransom for your Esmeralda.'

Wishing all pigs in Purgatory, I followed her down to the room at the end of the hall. A riveting sight met my gaze. A powerful, handsome young man and a portly, grizzled gentleman with a stethoscope round his neck were endeavouring to restrain some-one – this I took to be Monsieur Clot – who was desperately trying to rise from a recumbent position on a purple chaise-longue.

He was a tall man, slender as a minnow, wearing a black cor-duroy suit and a huge black beret. But his most striking attribute was his beard. Carefully nurtured, carefully cosseted and trimmed, it cascaded down as far as his navel and was a piebald mixture of black and iron grey hairs.

'Let me get at him, the misbegotten son of Satan,' Monsieur Clot was yelling, struggling to rise from the chaise-longue.

'Your heart, your heart, remember your heart,' shouted the doctor.

'Yes, yes, remember your heart,' shrieked Madame Clot.

'I will deal with him, Monsieur Clot,' said the handsome young man, glaring at me from ferocious gentian-blue eyes. He looked the sort of muscular young man who could bend horseshoes out of alignment with his little fingers.

'Let me get at him, let me tear out his jugular vein,' shouted Monsieur Clot, 'the illegitimate thief.'

'Your heart, your heart,' the doctor shouted.

'Henri, Henri, keep calm,' shrilled Madame Clot.

'I will disembowel him,' said the muscular young man.

The trouble with the French is that they love to talk but not to listen. One sometimes gets the very strong impression that they don't even listen to themselves. When you get embroiled in a turmoil of French citizens like this, there is only one thing to be done. You must out-shout them. Filling my lungs to the utmost capacity, I roared 'Silence' and silence fell as though I had waved a magic wand.

'Monsieur Clot,' I said, bowing to him, 'may I make it clear that I am not an assassin or a bandit and that I am not, to the best of my knowledge, illegitimate. Having said that, I feel I can vouchsafe to you the fact that I have in my possession a pig whose name is, I believe, Esmeralda.'

'Ahhhh!' cried Monsieur Clot, his worst fears confirmed.

'Silence!' I barked and he fell back on the chaise-longue with a delicate, slender and beautifully manicured hand spread, like a butterfly, over that portion of his anatomy in which he suspected his heart to have its abode.

'I met Esmeralda in the forest,' I continued. 'She shared my lunch with me and then, when I had ascertained in the village who her rightful owner was, I brought her back.'

'Esmeralda here? Esmeralda returned? Where? Where?' cried Monsieur Clot, struggling to rise.

'Slowly, slowly,' said the doctor. 'Remember your heart!'

'She is outside in my car,' I said.

'And . . . and . . . what ransom do you demand?' asked Monsieur Clot.

'I don't want a ransom,' I said.

Monsieur Clot and the doctor exchanged eloquent glances.

'No ransom?' said Monsieur Clot. 'She is an extremely valuable animal.'

'An animal beyond price,' said the doctor

'An animal worth five years' pay,' said the muscular young man.

'An animal worth more than La Reine Elizabeth's crown jewels,' said Madame Clot, bringing in the feminine angle with a touch of exaggeration to gild the lily.

'Nevertheless, I do not want a ransom,' I said, firmly. 'I am happy to return her to you.'

'No ransom?' said Monsieur Clot. He sounded almost insulted.

'No ransom,' I said.

Monsieur Clot glanced at the doctor who simply, palms out-stretched, shrugged and said, 'Voilà les Anglais.' Monsieur Clot shook himself free of both the doctor's and the muscular young man's grip and rose to his feet.

'Then, monsieur, I am deeply, deeply in your debt,' he said and snatched off his beret and placed it over his heart, his head bowed. Then he carefully replaced the beret on his head and ran across the room at me like a badly manipulated puppet and clasped me in his arms. His beard whispered like silk against my cheeks as he kissed me with all the vehemence that only a Frenchman can exhibit when kissing a member of the same sex.

'Mon brave, mon ami,' he said, clasping my shoulders, looking deeply into my eyes, the tears trickling like transparent tadpoles down his magnificent beard, 'take me to my beloved.'

So we went outside, woke Esmeralda and she climbed out of the car to be embraced, patted and kissed by everyone, including the doctor. Then we all – including Esmeralda – went back into the house where Monsieur Clot insisted on opening one of his best bottles of wine (a Château Montrose 1952) and we drank a toast to the pig of pigs who was being fed chocolate peppermints by Madame Clot.

'Monsieur Durrell,' said Monsieur Clot, 'you may think perhaps that we made a disproportionate amount of brouhaha over the disappearance of Esmeralda.'

'Not at all,' I said, 'it is most upsetting to lose such a fine pet.'

'She is more than just a pet,' said Monsieur Clot, in a hushed and reverent voice, 'she is the champion truffle pig of Périgord. Fifteen times she has won the silver cup for the most sensitive nose of any pig in the quartier. A truffle may lurk twenty centimetres beneath the forest floor and fifty metres away from Esmeralda and she will find it unerringly. She is like – she is like – well, she is like a pig Exocet.'

'Remarkable,' I said.

'Tomorrow morning at eight, if you will be so kind as to come, we will take Esmeralda into the forest and you shall see for yourself the powers that she possesses. And then if you would do us the honour of staying to lunch we should be delighted. I may say that my wife, Antoinette, is one of the finest cooks in the district.'

'Not only the finest cook, but the most beautiful,' said the doctor, gallantly.

'Yes, indeed,' said the muscular young man, fastening upon Madame Clot a look of such burning adoration that I was not surprised to learn that his name was Juan.

'I should be delighted and honoured,' I said and, finishing my wine, I took my leave.

The next morning was crisp and sunny, the sky as blue as a forget-me-not, the mist lying in tangled shawls among the trees. When I arrived at the farm, Monsieur Clot, in his disjointed way, was putting the final touches to Esmeralda's toilet. Her hooves had been rubbed with olive oil (the first pressing), she had been carefully brushed and special eye drops put in her tiny eyes. Then came the final touch. A minute phial of Joy was produced and a few drops were placed behind each of her drooping ears. Finally, a soft muzzle of chamois leather was put on her snout to discourage any inclination she might have to devour the truffles she found.

'Voilà,' said Monsieur Clot, triumphantly, waving his truffle spade. 'Now she is ready for the hunt.'

The next few hours were instructive, for I had never seen a truffle pig at work, least of all one so brilliantly versed in the art as Esmeralda. She walked through the oak forest that abutted Monsieur Clot's farm with all the slow dignity of an elderly opera singer making yet another farewell performance. As she walked, she crooned to herself in a series of falsetto grunts. Presently she stopped, lifted her head, eyes closed, and inhaled deeply. Then she walked to the base of a venerable oak and started to nose at the earth and leaf litter.

'She has found,' cried Monsieur Clot and, pushing Esmeralda to one side, he plunged his spade deeply into the forest floor. When the spade emerged it had balanced on it a truffle the size of a plum, black and redolent. Pungent and beautiful though the truffle scent was, I could not understand how Esmeralda, coated as she was in Joy, could detect the fungus' presence. However, to prove it was no fluke, during the next hour or so she found six more, each as rotund as the first. We carried these back in triumph to the farm and handed them over to Madame Clot who, her face flushed to a delicate pink, was busy in the kitchen. Esmeralda was put in her spotless pen and given her reward, a small baguette of bread split down the middle and stuffed with cheese, and Monsieur Clot and I regaled ourselves with Kir.

Presently, Madame called us to the table. Juan had – I think in my honour – put on a coat and tie and Monsieur Clot took off his beret. The first course, served in lovely earthenware bowls as thin, crisp and brown as autumn leaves, was a delicate chicken broth with fine fronds of onion and golden egg yolk swimming in it. This was followed by a plump trout, deboned and carefully stuffed with a mousseline of finely chopped chestnuts and fennel. Accompanying this were baby peas, sweet as sugar, and minute potatoes in a bath of mint. This had merely been the build-up to the final moment, the course we were all waiting for. Madame Clot cleared the plates away and put fresh ones, warm as newly baked loaves, in front of us. Monsieur Clot, with hushed ceremony, skilfully uncorked a Château Brane-Cantenac 1957, smelt the cork, slipped a few drops into a clean glass and savoured it for a moment. He reminded me, irresistibly, of Esmeralda with her cheese. He nodded his approval and then poured the wine, red as dragon's blood, into our glasses. At that moment, as if on cue, Madame made her entrance from the kitchen bearing a platter on which reposed four rounds of fragile pastry, yellow as ripe corn. One was carefully placed on each of our plates. We were all silent, as if in church. Slowly, Monsieur Clot raised his glass, toasted first his beautiful lady and then me and Juan. We all took a sip of wine and rolled it round our mouths, coating our taste buds in preparation. The knives and forks were lifted, the fragile shell of golden pastry flaked away, like the shell from a nut, and there lay the truffle, black as jet, and from the interior of the pastry came that incredible fragrance, the scent of a million autumnal forests, rich, mouth-watering and totally unlike any other taste or smell in the world. We ate in reverent silence, for even the French cease talking to eat. When the last morsel had melted in my mouth, I raised my glass.

'Madame Clot, Monsieur Clot, Juan, may I give you a toast. To Esmeralda, the finest pig in the world, a paragon of pigs.'

'Thank you, thank you, monsieur,' said Monsieur Clot, his voice trembling, his eyes filling with tears.

We had sat down to eat on the stroke of twelve for, as is well known in French medical circles, if lunch is delayed beyond midday it can prove instantly fatal to the French citizen. Such bounty had been spread before us by Madame Clot that, as I was finishing the greengage soufflé and cream, followed by a delectable Cantal cheese, I was not a bit surprised, on looking at my watch, to find that it was four o'clock. Refusing coffee and brandy, I said that I must go and that it had been the most memorable meal of my life. I asked and received permission to kiss Madame Clot's damask cheeks three times (once for God, once for the Virgin Mary, once for Jesus Christ, as someone had once told me), had my hand crushed by Juan, and was enveloped in Monsieur Clot's beard. Before I left he extracted a promise from me that, on my return, I would call in at the village and allow Madame Clot to cook me another meal, which I readily agreed to.

It was a year later that I was travelling down to the south of France and, as I approached the Périgord region, I remembered, with a guilty feeling, Monsieur Clot and Esmeralda and my promise to visit them. So I turned my car towards Petit Monbazillac-sur-Ruisseau and soon arrived at the Three Pigeons. Jean was overjoyed to see me.

'Monsieur Durrell,' he cried, 'we thought you had forgotten us. How wonderful to see you again.'

'Have you got a room for a couple of nights?' I asked.

'But certainly, monsieur,' he said, 'the best in the house.'

After he had installed me in a tiny but comfortable room and I had changed, I went down to the bar for a pastis.

'Tell me, how have things gone with you and my friends since I was last here?' I asked. 'How are Madame and Monsieur Clot and Esmeralda?'

Jean started and stared at me, his eyes bulging.

'Monsieur has not heard?' he asked.

'Heard? Heard what?' I asked. 'I've only just arrived.'

For all people who live in remote villages, the local news is of prime importance and for you to be ignorant of it is incomprehensible to them.

'It is terrible, terrible,' he said, with the relish of all who vouchsafe bad news. 'Monsieur Clot is in prison.'

'In prison!' I said, startled. 'Why, what has he done?'

'He fought a duel,' said Jean.

'Monsieur Clot fought a *duel*?' I said in amazement. 'With whom, for heaven's sake?'

'With Juan,' said Jean.

'But why?'

'Because Juan ran away with Madame Clot,' said Jean.

'How incredible,' I said, feeling privately that it was not that incredible, since Juan was a handsome lad and Monsieur Clot was approaching seventy.

'Worse was to follow,' said Jean, lowering his voice to a conspiratorial whisper.

'Worse?'

'Worse.'

'What could be worse than running off with another man's wife!' I queried.

'A week after they had disappeared, Juan came back and stole Esmeralda.'

'Never!' I cried.

'Yes, monsieur. Juan is, of course, a Spaniard,' said Jean, as if that explained everything.

'What happened then?'

'Monsieur Clot, as a man of honour and bravery should, followed them and challenged Juan to a duel. Juan comes from Toledo so naturally he chose rapiers. Little did he know that, in his youth, Monsieur Clot used to be a champion of the foil. So, within seconds, Monsieur Clot had stabbed Juan through his chest, just missing his heart. For days, Juan's life hung in the balance, but now he is starting to recover.'

'When did all this happen?'

'Last week, and they have Monsieur Clot in the prison at Sainte-Justine awaiting trial.'

'The poor man. I must go and see him,' I said.

'He will be most enchanted to see you, Monsieur,' said Jean,

So the following day I went to the prison, bearing the only gift you can give a Frenchman incarcerated in a jail on a charge of attempted murder, a bottle of J & B whisky.

He was sitting on the edge of the iron bedstead in his cell, reading a book. He was, alas, no longer the immaculate Monsieur Clot I had known. His shirt with no collar was prison issue, as were the thin frayed cotton pants and the slippers. There was no tie or belt with which he might have been tempted to commit suicide, should he have been the sort of man to contemplate such a deed. However, his hair was as immaculate as ever, as was his splendid beard, carefully combed and cosseted. The slender fingers that held the book were spotlessly clean and as carefully manicured as always.

'Here's a visitor for you, Monsieur Clot,' said the warder, unlocking the barred door. Monsieur Clot looked up in astonishment and then his face lit up as he laid the book hastily aside and leapt to his feet.

'Why, Monsieur Durrell,' he cried, delightedly, 'what a surprise – what an honour – how wonderful to see you.

He clasped my hand in both his, a perhaps unwise move since, as he leant forward to embrace me, it allowed his trousers to descend concertina-wise to his ankles. But even this catastrophe could not dampen his spirits.

'These fools think that I am going to kill myself with my belt.

I ask you, Monsieur Durrell, would a man of my reputation, of my standing in the community a man of education and no little renown, stoop to such a vulgar deed, the cowardly action of an artisan of the lower orders? – Parraf!' he said, and with a courteous old world gesture indicated that I might sit on the bed.

'It is so good to see you,' he continued, 'even in these less than salubrious surroundings. It is so very generous of you to come. So many people in your position would have hesitated to visit a man in jail, even one of my reputation.'

'Not at all,' I said, 'I came as soon as I heard from Jean. I'm very distressed by the whole thing.'

'Indeed, indeed,' he said, nodding portentously, his beard rippling. 'I myself am greatly distressed. I hate doing a job badly, it is not in my nature and I feel my failure deeply.'

'Your failure?' I said, confused. 'What failure?'

'My failure to kill him, of course,' said Monsieur Clot, his eyes widening in astonishment that I should not have perceived this glaring fault.

'Surely you can't mean that?' I said.

'I do,' he said firmly. 'I wish that my aim had been true and that I had killed him outright – PARRAF!'

'But Monsieur Clot, if you had killed him you would stand no chance of getting off. As it is I am sure it will be treated as a crime of passion and you will only get a light sentence.'

'A crime of passion? I do not understand,' said Monsieur Clot.

'Well, he enticed away your very beautiful wife, and that, I would say, was sufficient reason for acting as you did.'

'You think I fought a duel, risked my life for my wife?' he asked in astonishment.

'Well, didn't you?' I asked, puzzled.

'No,' he said flatly, banging his fist on the bed. 'I did not.'

'Then why on earth did you fight the duel?' I asked.

'For my pig of course, for Esmeralda,' he said.

'For your *pig*?' I asked incredulously. 'Not your wife?' Monsieur Clot leant forward and looked at me very seriously.

'Monsieur Durrell, listen to me. A man can always replace a wife, but a good truffle pig – like Esmeralda – impossible!' he said, with great conviction.

Fred — or A Touch of the Warm South

I have on two occasions ventured – very unwisely – on lecture tours in the United States of America. While thus engaged, I fell deeply in love with Charleston and San Francisco, hated Los Angeles – a misnomer if ever there was one – was exhilarated by New York and loathed Chicago and St Louis. During the course of my peregrinations many strange things befell me but it was not until I ventured south of the Mason-Dixon line that I had my strangest experience of all. I had been asked by the Literary Guild of Memphis, Tennessee, to lecture them on conservation. The Guild informed me, with a certain amount of smug satisfaction, that I was to stay with no less exalted a person than the deputy treasurer, a Mrs Magnolia Dwite-Henderson. Now, when I go a-lecturing, I hate being a guest at a stranger's house. All too often they say to me, 'Now you've been on the road for the last three weeks and we know you must be simply exhausted, worn out, debilitated. Well, with us you're going to have a *real* rest. This evening we're only going to have forty of our most intimate friends to dinner, whom you will simply *adore*. Just a quiet relaxed gathering of the people we love, but who are simply crazy to meet you. One of them has even read your books.'

Knowing from bitter experience that this can and does happen, I felt a certain alarm at the Literary Guild farming me out to Mrs Magnolia Dwite-Henderson. So I phoned her up in the hopes that I could somehow, as politely as possible, get out of staying with her and go to an hotel instead. A deep rich voice answered the telephone, the sort of voice a vintage port would have if it could speak.

'Dis here is Miz Magnolia's residence,' it intoned. 'Who is dat what ahm talking to?'

'My name is Durrell and I would like to speak to Mrs Dwite Henderson,' I said.

'Yew jus' hold on to dat line,' said the voice, 'en I'll go seek her out.'

There was a long pause and then a breathless tinkly voice, like a musical box, came on the line.

'Mister Dewrell, is that yew?' it asked. 'This is Magnolia Dwite-Henderson speaking to yew.'

'I'm delighted to have this chance to talk to you, Mrs Dwite-Henderson,' I said.

'Oh mercy me,' she shrilled, 'your ac-cent, your AC-cent – it's the most perfect thing I've ever heard. It's just like talking to Sir Laurence Olivier. I do declare it sends shivers up mah spine.'

'Thank you,' I said. 'I have just heard from the Guild that they have more or less forced you to put me up. Now, I do think this is a great imposition and I would much rather stay in an hotel and not inconvenience you in this way.'

'Inconvenience me?' she squeaked. 'Why, honey lamb, it's an *honour* to have yew in the house. I wouldn't let yew stay in a hotel where they never sweep under the beds or empty the ashtrays. It would be going against the grain of true Southern hospitality. I wouldn't even let a Yankee stay in a hotel if he was coming to lecture – not that they have much to lecture about. They are all wind and water as my father used to say, only he used a stronger word.'

My heart sank. I could see that no way was I going to get out of staying with Mrs Dwite-Henderson without offending Southern hospitality.

'You're very kind,' I said. 'My plane gets in at half past four so I should be with you by five.'

'Wonderful!' she said. 'Yew'll be just in time for my special tea – every Thursday I have five of my dearest friends to tea and, of course, they are simply on tenterhooks to meet yew.'

With an effort I suppressed a groan.

'Well, I'll see you at five then,' I said.

'I cain't wait till yew get hayer,' she said.

I put down the phone and went to catch my plane with some misgivings. Two hours later I was in the deep South, the land of cotton, black-eyed peas, sweet potatoes and – unfortunately Elvis Presley. I was propelled from the airport in a taxi driven by a very large man smoking a large cigar roughly the colour of his skin.

'Yew from Boston?' he enquired, after we had travelled some way.

'No,' I said, 'why would you think that?'

'Axe-cent,' he said succinctly, 'your axe-cent.'

'No,' I said, 'I'm from England.'

'Dat right?' he said. 'England, eh?'

'Yes,' I said.

'How's de Queen doing?' he asked.

'I think she's doing real fine,' I said, endeavouring to enter into the spirit of the deep South.

'Yeah,' he said reflectively, 'she's some woman, dat Queen she's got a lot of balls ah reckon.'

I remained silent. As a commentary on the royal family, I felt his remark said it all.

The residence of Mrs Magnolia Dwite-Henderson was a sort of dwarfed old style colonial mansion set in two acres of carefully manicured garden, with white colonnades standing shoulder to shoulder with vast quantities of purple azaleas. The front door, which must have measured twelve feet by four, had an enormous brass knocker that was so polished it gleamed as if it were on fire. As the taxi drew up this handsome door was thrown open to frame a very large, very black gentleman with white hair in tail coat and striped trousers. He looked as though he might be the accredited Ambassador of practically any emerging nation. In the rich port-like tones that I remembered from the telephone he said, 'Mr Dewrell, welcome to Miz Magnolia's residence,' and then added as an afterthought, 'Ahyam Fred.'

'Glad to know you, Fred,' I said. 'Can you handle the luggage?'

'Everything will be under control,' said Fred.

The taxi driver had deposited my two suitcases on the gravel and driven off. Fred surveyed them as if they were offensive litter.

'Fred,' I said, interested, 'do you normally wear that clothing?' He glanced down his body with disdain.

'No,' he said, 'but Miz Magnolia say ah was to greet yew in traditional costume.'

'You mean that this is traditional costume here in Memphis?' I asked.

'No suh,' he said bitterly, 'it's traditional costume where yew comes from.'

I sighed.

'Fred,' I said, 'do me a favour. Go and take off those garments. I am flattered that you put them on for me but I shall be even more flattered if you take them off for me and you will be more comfortable.'

A great smile appeared on his face. It was as though you had briefly lifted the lid on a grand piano.

'Ah sure will do dat, Mr Dewrell,' he said thankfully.

I entered the cool hall which smelt of furniture polish, flowers and herbs and Miz Magnolia came pitter-pattering down the parquet to greet me, like a thread of smoke clad in chiffon and scent, tinkling with jewels, fragile as a will-o'-the-wisp, blue eyes big as saucers, the delicate skin of her throat hanging down like victory banners of her successful survival. Under her eyes hung pouches as big as swallows' nests, her face was a network of wrinkles as intricate as any spider's web and her hair was that extraordinary shade of electric blue that many American women obtain when they have reluctantly tiptoed from the forties into the fifties.

'Mr Dewrell,' she said, clasping my hand in both of her fragile ones, which appeared to be made out of chicken bones and fine parchment. 'Mr Dewrell, yew are so welcome, suh. It is an Honour to have yew in the house.'

'It's an honour to be here, mam,' I said.

Fred loomed up suddenly like a large and ominous black cloud on a sunny afternoon.

'Miz Magnolia,' he announced. 'Ah is goin' to take mah clothes off.'

'Fred!' she said, shocked. 'I do not think that is wise or decent.'

'Mr Dewrell said ah could,' said Fred, thus implicating me.

'Oh!' said Miz Magnolia, startled. 'Well, I suppose that's different. But I am sure Mr Dewrell did not want you to take off your clothes this very instant. Not hayer, at any rate, where Great Aunt Dorinda might see.'

'Ah is goin' to do it private in mah own room,' said Fred, and stalked off.

'Now, why in the world would he want to disrobe?' asked Miz Magnolia. 'Yew know, the longer yew live with people the more complicated they become.'

I began to have that *Alice in Wonderland* feeling that I always get when entering Greece. You have to toss logic overboard and let it float – but at a retrievable distance – for a short time. I find it does wonders for the brain cells.

'Mr Dewrell, honey lamb,' she said, clasping my hand more firmly, 'yew must be simply *perishing* for want of a drink.'

'Well, that would be nice,' I said. 'A tiny Scotch and . . .'

'Shhhhh,' she said, 'Fred might hayer. He's so against drinking since he married again and joined this new Second Revelation Church. You have no idea. He does nothing but go about saying that strong drink is raging and accusing everyone of fornication – even me. Now I am the first one to admit that in MAH time I was a bit of a flirt but I do assure yew that fornication never entered mah hayed. Mr Dwite-Henderson would never have allowed it. He was all for virginity.'

My ideas of a Bloody Mary faded. She led me into the living room and then hastened to the handsome drink cabinet.

'A drink,' she said. 'A drink for flagging spirits.'

She opened the cabinet and to my alarm it contained nothing but opened bottles of Coca-Cola.

'What would yew like?' she asked me in a husky whisper. 'Vodka, whisky bourbon, gin?'

'I'd like a Scotch,' I said, somewhat startled.

She ran her finger along the Coca-Cola bottles and finally chose one, smelt it and poured a heavy measure into a glass, added ice and a dash of Perrier and handed it to me.

'The best sort of Coca-Cola,' she said smiling, 'and it doesn't upset Fred.'

The Scotch was excellent.

I went upstairs, showered and changed and started down to face Miz Magnolia's tea party.

A door on the landing opened and a tall, cadaverous-looking man emerged, wearing a black velvet dressing gown with scarlet piping and a Panama hat.

'Sir, is there any news?' he asked me.

'About what?' I asked.

'About the war, sir, the war. Mark my words, it will be a sad day for the South if they win,' he said, and turning he went back into his room and closed the door.

I continued, somewhat mystified, downstairs.

'Oh, you darling man,' said Miz Magnolia, engulfing me in a frail embrace of sweetly smooth rustling garments and a scent that made the senses reel. 'I am so happy to have you hayer. And *I know* that you are going to be so *happy* to meet mah dearest and loveliest friends.'

They came in as animals were supposed to come into the Ark, two by two. Miz Magnolia presented them rather in the way that a ringmaster of a circus would.

'Now, this is Miz Florence Further Cause. The Further Causes are, of course, widely known.'

When five of them were clustered together it gave me the feeling of an animated flowerbed talking a language you don't know. 'This,' said Miz Magnolia, 'is Marigold Nasta . . .'

I bowed gravely.

'And this is Miz Melancholy Delight.'

I took an instant liking to Miss Melancholy Delight. She looked like a bulldog who has – by mistake – been put through a washing machine. Nevertheless, I felt that any woman who had survived through life being called Melancholy Delight demanded my masculine support.

They were all magical. Fragile as anything an archaeologist can produce from the tombs of Egypt, twittering like birds, as conscious of themselves as girls at their first ball. But having got over the excitement and gravity of my intrusion they reverted to the smooth rolling way of life they were used to.

'Did you hayer about Gray-ham?' one of them asked.

They all leant forward like vultures seeing a movement from a lion who might leave his kill.

'What about Gray-ham?' they all asked with relish.

'Well, Gray-ham has run away with Patsy Donahue.'

'He hasn't!'

'He has.'

'He hasn't!'

'He has, and left that adorable girl Hilda on her own with three children.'

'Hilda was a Watson wasn't she, before she married?'

'Yes, but the Watsons were a mixed-up bunch. Old grand pappy Watson married that Ferguson girl.'

'You mean the Fergusons who lived out near Mud Island?'

'No, no, these are the Fergusons from East Memphis. Their grandmother was a Scott before she married Mr Ferguson and their aunt was related to the Tellymares.'

'You don't mean old man Tellymare who committed suicide?'

'No, that was his cousin, Arthur, the one with a limp. That was in 1914.'

It was like listening to an amalgam of the *Almanae de Gotha*, *Debrett*, and the *Social Register* being read aloud simultaneously. These old ladies could track everyone and their antecedents back to the fifth generation and beyond with the tenacity of bloodhounds. Gray-ham and his misdemeanour with Patsy were now lost in a genealogical confusion with all the complications of a plate of spaghetti.

'It was Tellymare's cousin Albert who was married to that

Nancy Henderson girl who divorced him because he set fire to himself,' said Miz Melancholy Delight.

The group took this extraordinary piece of information in their stride.

'Wasn't she one of the Henderson twins, the ones with red hayer and all those unsightly freckles?'

'Yes, and their cousin married the Breverton man and then shot him,' said Miz Marigold.

'A most unsatisfactory family,' said Miz Magnolia. 'I'll go and get the tea.'

She reappeared in a moment bearing a large silver tray on which reposed a gigantic silver teapot, delicate china cups and two silver dishes, one containing ice cubes and the other sliced lemon.

'There's nothing like tea on a hot day like this,' said Miz Magnolia, putting lemon and ice cubes into a cup and handing it to me. I took it, wondering why all the ladies were watching me with an air of expectancy. I raised the cup to my lips, took a sip and choked. The cup contained straight bourbon.

'Is it to your liking?' asked Miz Magnolia.

'Excellent,' I said. 'I take it that Fred didn't make it.'

'Oh, no,' said Miz Magnolia, smiling, 'I always make the tea mahself. It saves trouble, yew know.'

'Mah pappy always say-ed to me that cold tea helped the flesh,' said Miz Marigold, somewhat mysteriously.

'Little Miz Lillibut – you remember she was married to Hubert Crumb, one of those Crumbs from Mississippi, who were related by marriage to the Ostlers,' said Miz Melancholy, 'well, she always washed her face in iced tea and she had a complexion like a peach, a veritable peach.'

'Miz Ruby Mackintosh – she was one of the Scottish Mackintoshes that came over from Scotland and married into the Mackinnon family, and old man Mackinnon was such a bully he drove his wife into the grave – she was a Tenderson girl, whose mother was an Outgrabe from Minnesota – well Miz Ruby always say-ed that there was nothing like cream and pecan oil for the skin,' said Miz Marigold.

27

'Weren't the Mackintoshes related to the Quinsers?' asked Miz Magnolia.

'Yes, Miz Ruby's uncle married a Quinser, the one with the fallen arches and a figger like a sack of sweet potatoes,' said Miz Melancholy.

I decided to cut across this genealogical reverie.

'Miz Melancholy,' I said, 'you have such an attractive name. How did you come by it?'

She looked at me, puzzled.

'Baptism,' she said at last.

'But who chose your name?' I asked.

'Mah father,' she said. 'You see, he wanted a boy.'

Another hour went by in a haze of bourbon and a patchwork of names and families. Finally, the ladies rose to take their unsteady departure.

'Well,' said Miz Magnolia, when they had vanished in a flurry of kisses and 'loved seeing yew'. 'I'm going to come up and see your room.'

'But my room's fine,' I protested. 'It's absolutely wonderful.'

'I like to check things for mahself,' said Miz Magnolia ominously. 'Now Fred's turned eighty-nine he's not as observant as he used to be.'

'Eighty-nine?' I asked incredulously.

'Certainly is,' said Miz Magnolia, starting up the stairs. 'He'll be ninety on December 22nd.'

Before I could comment on this, the gentleman in the velvet dressing gown appeared at the head of the stairs waving a large and extremely sharp-looking sabre.

'They're burning Atlanta,' he shouted.

'Mercy me,' said Miz Magnolia, 'he has been watching that darned video of *Gone with the Wind* again. I wish Cousin Cuthbert hadn't given it to him at Christmas.'

'They'll be hayer any minute,' shouted the man with the sabre. 'Can I introduce you to Great Uncle Rochester,' said Miz Magnolia.

'Have you buried the silver?' asked Great Uncle Rochester. 'There's not much time.'

I remembered that during the Civil War the Southerners spent a lot of their spare time burying the family silver in case it was looted by the damned Yankees.

'Yes, yes, honey lamb, don't fret. I buried the silver,' said Miz Magnolia, soothingly.

'They'll be hayer any minute,' repeated Great Uncle Rochester. 'We'll fight to the last man.'

'You have no reason to discompose yourself,' said Miz Magnolia. 'I have a personal assurance from General Jackson they will not take Memphis.'

'Jackson?' said Great Uncle Rochester with scorn. 'I wouldn't believe him if he told me I was Lincoln.'

I felt this observation confused the issue somewhat.

'Well he told *me*,' said Miz Magnolia, 'and surely to heaven you trust *me*?'

'You didn't tell me I was Lincoln,' said Great Uncle Rochester with a sudden flash of perspicacity.

Great Uncle Rochester, to my alarm, whirled the sabre in the air, caught it deftly by the blade and handed it to me hilt first.

'You take the first watch,' he said. 'Wake me at midnight or before if necessary.'

'You may rely on me, sir,' I said.

'We must fight to the death,' he said gravely, and stalked off into his room and slammed the door.

'Now we can go and inspect your room,' said Miz Magnolia happily. 'I would put that nasty sword thing under your bed if I were yew. Sometimes the cats make a lot of noise in the garden and it is a useful thing to throw.'

Miz Magnolia minutely examined my room and found it to her satisfaction.

'Now,' she said, 'I must go and examine the hall.'

'The hall?' I said, puzzled.

'The hall where yew are going to speak,' she said. 'If I don't examine it there is always a disconambulation. There was one poor man who had all his slides in upside down. It was a very confused lecture.'

'I would prefer for that not to happen to me,' I said, 'if that can be avoided.'

'Yew just sit yourself in the living room,' she said, 'and have a nice drink of Coca-Cola. I'll be back directly.'

So I sat in the living room with a weak bourbon and read the local paper. Suddenly, a small, rotund old lady with vivid blue hair made her appearance on the stairs, wearing a voluminous green dressing gown so covered in cigarette burns it looked as though it was made of lace. Humming to herself she descended the stairs and gave a yelp of fright as I got to my feet and she saw me.

'Mercy me!' she squeaked, holding her clasped hands to her ample bosom.

'I'm sorry if I startled you,' I said. 'My name's Durrell and I'm staying here.'

'Oh, you're the Englishman who's come to lecture us,' she said, smiling. 'Ah'm so glad to meet you. Ah'm Great Aunt Dorinda.'

'A great pleasure, madam,' I said.

'Ah just came down for a Coca-Cola,' she said, floating across to the drinks cabinet. She sniffed all the Coca-Cola bottles until she found one to her liking.

'Ah'll just take it upstairs,' she said. 'Ah'm so sorry mah husband Mr Rochester is not here at the moment, but he's out fighting the war – such a noisy business. But he'll be back directly when he's won it. Ah'm not sure how long it will take. Ah don't really know very much about these masculine pursuits, but it seems to make them happy and that's the main thing, don't yew think?'

'Indeed I do, madam,' I said.

'But as ah say, he'll be back presently. Ah'm not sure when, of course. I believe some wars take longer than others,' she said vaguely.

'So I am led to believe,' I agreed.

'Well, do make yourself at home,' she said and giving me a shy smile, and clutching her Coca-Cola bottle she drifted upstairs. Somewhat shaken by this encounter I poured myself another bourbon and, finding no ice in the cooler, I went out to the back regions where I presumed Fred had his abode.

I found him in a green baize apron sitting at the kitchen table which was covered with such an enormous pile of silver it would have made Captain Kidd blink.

'Ah am cleaning de silver,' he said unnecessarily.

'So I see,' I said. 'Could I have some ice?'

'Yes, suh,' he said, 'you sho' can. Ain't nothin' worse than warm Coca-Cola.'

He fetched the ice cubes and put them in my drink.

'Yes, suh, it's nice to live in a house with no strong liquor. Strong drink is raging.'

He picked up a silver dish in which you could have easily bathed a baby and started to polish it. I sipped my bourbon furtively.

'Take a seat, suh,' said Fred, hospitably, drawing out a stool. 'Take a seat and set awhile.'

'Thank you,' I said, sitting down and hoping the strong smell of liquor would not drift across the table to Fred's nostrils.

'Are you a religious man?' he asked, busy with polishing silver so bright that it did not seem in need of it.

'Church of England,' I said.

'Is dat right?' said Fred. 'Dat would be in England, wouldn't it?'

'Yes,' I said.

'Is dat anywhere near de Pope?' asked Fred.

'No, a fair distance away.'

'Dat Pope's always kissing de ground,' said Fred, shaking his head. 'Ah don't know why he don't have a disease, carrying on like dat.'

'It's a habit Popes have,' I explained.

'It's a *bad* habit,' said Fred firmly. 'It's not clean. He don't know who's bin there before him.'

He picked up a salver big enough to accommodate the head of John the Baptist and started work on it.

'Ah was never a religious man until I was saved by Charity,' he remarked.

'By Charity?' I asked, puzzled.

'Mah third wife,' he explained. 'She introduced me to the Church of the Second Revelation en ah become saved. It was all explained to me. All de woes of de world you can blame on one woman.'

'Who?' I asked, hoping he was not going to say Miz Magnolia.

'Eve,' he said, 'dat who. She was de one what created strong liquor and fornication.'

'How did she invent strong liquor?' I enquired, feeling that, if true, this was a point in Eve's favour rather than the reverse.

'Apples,' said Fred. 'Dat tree of knowledge got apples on it en where yew got apples yew can be sure they're gonna make cider. En she was probably drunk to do what she did.'

'What did she do?' I asked, now thoroughly mystified.

'She was dislocated in her brain by drink,' said Fred with conviction. 'What woman in her right mind gonna talk to a snake? No, a normal woman would-a gone a-running and phoned up de police and de fire brigade.'

I had a momentary but very clear vision of the Garden of Eden with half a dozen bright red fire-engines and a covey of policemen surrounding the Tree of the Knowledge of Good and Evil.

'Yes, and den she was de cause of all de overpopulation we got now, yes siree.'

'But Eve didn't have many children,' I protested.

'But what did *dey* do?' he asked. 'What did dey do, eh? Fornication – if yew'll excuse the word. Fornication left right and centre. Stand to reason all dat begetting gonna lead to overpopulation. Yes, fornication and cider, dat's why de good Lord expelled dem.'

I must say this gave me a completely new slant on the downfall of Adam and Eve.

'If they'd had prohibition in those days it might of helped,' Fred continued, 'but even de good Lord couldn't think of *everything*.'

'I suppose not,' I said thoughtfully.

My ecclesiastical investigations with Fred were, to my sorrow, cut short by the arrival of Miz Magnolia, who came bustling in to tell me that the hall was not in any way, shape or form disconambulated, and that the cream of Memphis society would be expecting me on stage in an hour's time.

'You have just time for a Coca-Cola,' she said coyly.

It seemed to me that since my arrival in Memphis I had done nothing but imbibe the Demon Drink in vast quantities, but nevertheless I had one more heart-warming libation before my appearance.

My lecture was a wild success. Not, I fear, because of its riveting content but because of my axe-cent.

'Your axe-cent is really something else,' said a large, red-faced, white-whiskered man to me afterwards. 'It's really and truly, sir, something else. It's surely exciting, you know – like that guy, what's his name – yes, William Shakespeare.'

'Thank you,' I said.

'Have you ever thought of moving down South and becoming an American?' he asked. 'With an axe-cent like yours we'd surely welcome yew.'

I said that I was gratified; the thought had not occurred to me, but I would bear it in mind.

The next morning, suffering I regret to say from a hangover, due to over-indulgence in Southern hospitality, I made my way in a somewhat fragile state downstairs to breakfast, where I found them all assembled round a highly polished table, glittering with silver like a mountain brook, and Fred in attendance.

'Oh,' said Great Aunt Dorinda, 'this is mah husband Mr Rochester.'

'We have met, Dorinda,' said Great Uncle Rochester. 'This gallant gentleman helped me fend off the rebel horde of Yankees last night.'

'That must have been nice for yew both,' said Aunt Dorinda. 'Ah do think it's lovely when yew can share things together.'

'Did you get a good night's sleep?' asked Miz Magnolia, ignoring the other two.

'Splendid,' I said, as Fred helped me to a tiny Southern breakfast of six slices of bacon, crisp and fragrant as autumn leaves, four eggs, gleaming like newly emerged suns, eight pieces of toast engulfed in butter and a large, glittering, trembling spoonful of lemon preserve.

'I am going to get the latest news,' said Great Uncle Rochester, rising and drawing his dressing gown around him.

'Will yew be back for lunch or still fighting?' asked Great Aunt Dorinda.

'Madam, a war cannot be hurried,' said Great Uncle Rochester, sternly.

'No, no, ah realize that,' said Great Aunt Dorinda, 'but ah just wanted to know about the ice cream.'

'There are more important things on my mind, woman, than ice cream,' said Great Uncle Rochester. 'Is it vanilla or strawberry?'

'Strawberry?' said Great Aunt Dorinda.

'I'll have two scoops and some nutcake,' said Great Uncle Rochester, and took his leave of us, while Great Aunt Dorinda went to the kitchen.

'Ah do declare, ah do not know what things are coming to,' said Miz Magnolia, perusing the local paper. 'Now they've got a nigger they want to make the mayor.'

I glanced uneasily at the door through which Fred had disappeared.

'If you ask my opinion, we are ruled by a bunch of white trash and niggers – we really are – white trash and niggers,' she said, sipping her coffee.

'Tell me, Miz Magnolia, in view of the sensitivity of black people today, do you think it wise to talk like that when Fred's about?' I asked.

'Talk like what?' she said, turning enormous puzzled eyes on me.

'Well, talking about niggers and so on.'

'But Fred's not a nigger,' she said indignantly.

I wondered for a brief moment if she was, perhaps, colour-blind.

'No,' she continued. 'My great-grandfather bought Fred's grandfather back 1850. Ah've still got the receipt. Fred was born here. Fred's no nigger. Fred's family.'

I gave up trying to understand the Southern mind.

Retirement

In my travels I have met with many events that have saddened and distressed me. But of this multitude of happenings there is one incident that is engraved on my mind and fills me with sorrow whenever I think of it.

He was a very small man with no more bulk than a forlorn fourteen-year-old boy. His bones seemed as fragile and delicate as the stems of ancient clay pipes. He had a strange head perched on his slender neck like a Greek amphora upside down. In this were framed gigantic liquid eyes the size and shape of a doe's, a nose as finely chiselled as a bird's wing and a mouth beautifully formed, generous and compassionate. His ears, delicate as parchment, were large and pointed as a pixie's are supposed to be. He was the Scandinavian Captain of the merchant vessel we were travelling on from Australia to Europe.

In those lovely far-off days you could travel on such vessels, which took six weeks and carried only eight or maybe twelve passengers. This was no QE2. It was really like having your own personal yacht. However, it had its pitfalls because you could not choose your fellow passengers. But out of twelve you were sure to meet at least two who vaguely resembled the human race and with whom you could strike up a friendship and thus ignore the others without causing offence. On this particular occasion I was the only male passenger on board. The other eleven were elderly Australian ladies who – with much twittering and excitement – were venturing on their very first voyage on a ship, their very first trip to Europe and their very first venture to the homeland of England where the Queen lives. So, as may be imagined, everything was so new and exciting to them that it had to be crooned over. The cabins were wonderful, with real beds, the showers and baths had real water, in the saloon they were served with real drinks and at meals they sat at a large table (polished) while they were served real food. They were like children at their first picnic and it was a joy to watch their enjoyment. However, the source of their most profound enjoyment was the Captain. They took one look at him and fell immediately, deeply, seriously and irrevocably in love with him. For his part, the Captain displayed such charm and consideration that he became, instantly, a sort of nautical Pied Piper. He would go the rounds of everybody basking in deck-chairs to check that the breakfast had been to their liking, that the beef tea (served at eleven o'clock precisely) had been of the right temperature, later in the saloon he would personally attend to the rites so necessary for fabricating that nauseating drink, the dry martini. He would send sailors a-running to alert the ladies to a flock of flying fish, a whale spouting like a fountain in the distance or an albatross floating on ruler-taut wings at our stern as if pinned there to an invisible wire. He took them up to the bows (with an escort of crew members to ensure nobody fell) to watch the dolphins keeping pace with the ship or suddenly zooming ahead in a breathtaking burst of speed and then throwing themselves out of the blue water like exuberant arrows. He took them down to the glittering engine room, where you could have eaten off the floor, and explained to them the internal organs of a ship. He took them up to the bridge from which the ship was run and explained how radar could let you be a ship that passed in the night and not a nasty accident. He took them down to the kitchens and the deep freezes, showing them where the food for their meals was kept and prepared, and they were enchanted. With each revelation they became more and more deeply in love with the Captain and he, enchanting, shy, tender little man that he was, strove each day to produce more and more amazing things for his ladies as a conjuror will produce more and more surprises out of his hat to amaze you.

'The Captain's got an 'art of gold,' the large and forever perspiring Mrs Farthingale said to me over the morning's beef tea, 'just pure gold. If my husband had been more like that, perhaps our marriage would 'ave lasted.'

Not having known the redoubtable Mr Farthingale, I could pass no comment.

'The Captain's the sweetest man I ever met, the very soul of courtesy and kindness and such good manners for a foreigner,' said Miss Landlock, her eyes filling with tears that threatened to overflow into her second martini. 'And happily married, so the Chief Officer tells me.'

'Yes,' I said, 'so I believe.'

She sighed lugubriously.

'All nice ones are,' she said.

'Yes,' said Mrs Fortescue, well into her third gin, poured with a generous hand, 'there are too few decent blokes around without wives. As soon as I saw the Captain, I said to myself, now there's a good bloke, not one to go philandering even if he is a sailor.'

'The Captain would never philander,' said Miss Woodbye, rather shocked. 'He's too much of a gentleman.'

'If his wife caught him philandering she'd be spitting chips she'd be that annoyed,' said Miss Landlock.

As there was little to do on the ship and the voyage was a long one, I was treated each day to endless speculation about the Captain's habits, admiration for his many virtues and advice as to what they should buy him as a present when we got to our first (and only) port of call. They looked forward to this day with great eagerness – not, I think, because they wanted to go ashore, but in order to purchase their hero's gift. After much argument, it was decided to buy him a sweater. As the price of such a garment was in doubt, it was decided that each lady was to give two pounds and I, nobly, said I would make up any difference. Having settled this thorny problem amicably, instant warfare broke out when we came to the problem of colour. White was impractical, red was too garish, brown was too sombre, green did not match his eyes and so on, interminably. In the end, before the ladies actually came to blows over this issue, I said that I, with the extraordinary cunning I used to entrap the wild denizens of the jungle, would extract from the Captain his favourite colour. When I eventually returned with the entirely spurious news that the Captain liked oatmeal, the ladies were disappointed but took it well. Another world war had been averted.

Eventually the great day dawned and the ship put into port. The ladies had been up at dawn, as excited as children on Christmas morning. They had been flitting from cabin to cabin in their dressing gowns with shrill cries of 'Marjorie, have you got a safety pin you could lend me?' 'Agatha, do you think these beads will go with my blue?' or 'You couldn't lend me a bra, could you – this one's gone and broken its strap.' Eventually, clad in their best, straw hats ablaze with artificial flowers, so redolent with powder and perfume that they could be smelt a hundred yards upwind, their eyes shining, their faces wreathed in excited smiles, they were all packed like a flowerbed into the tender and set off for shore and their great adventure.

In spite of their pleas and entreaties, I had decided not to go with them. It was a wise decision, for the idea – although I did not tell them this – of going shopping with eleven women, all hell bent on getting the best for their idol, filled me with alarm. Besides, I was in the middle of a book and so I thought I would work quietly in my cabin and order a drink and a sandwich for lunch. Unfortunately, it was not to be. I had barely started work when there was a knock on the cabin door. It was the Chief Officer. He was a man of about thirty, I suppose, with tightly clipped corn-gold hair, a rather heavy face and blue eyes without any expression in them. He had always struck me as being polite, efficient, but a bit on the dour side, compared with the captain's charming personality.

'The Captain's compliments,' he said. 'He did not see you going ashore with the ladies. The Captain wishes to know if you are unwell?'

'No, I'm perfectly well, thank you. I just decided to stay on board and finish my work.'

'Then the Captain says will you do him the honour of having lunch with him?'

I was somewhat taken aback, but there was really nothing I could do but accept.

'Tell the Captain I will be delighted,' I said.

'Quarter to one in the bar,' said the Chief Officer, and went off.

So at quarter to one I drifted into the bar to find the Captain sipping at a glass of pale sherry, with a whole pile of parchment-like papers on the bar in front of him. He shook my hand formally, ordered me a drink and then perched back on his stool, like a pixie on a mushroom top.

'As soon as I saw you were not going ashore,' he said, 'I felt I must ask you to lunch. I did not like to think of you lunching alone.'

'You are most kind, Captain,' I said. 'As a matter of fact, the reason I did not go ashore is because our ladies wanted to do some shopping. I felt that to spend the day shopping with eleven ladies would be more than my nerves could stand.'

'Just shopping with one lady is a bad experience, I think. When my wife goes shopping I never accompany her. She brings everything back to the house to show me and the next day she takes it all back to change it,' he said. 'But ladies are ladies and we could not do without them.'

'My brother, who has been married four times, once said to me: "Couldn't they have invented something better than women?"'

At this the Captain laughed so heartily that he almost fell off his bar stool. When he had recovered and we had ordered more drinks, he became serious.

'It is about the ladies I wish to consult you, Mr Durrell,' he said. 'As you know, in four days' time we will be crossing the Equator and we must have a Crossing the Line Ceremony. It will be expected. Now, if you have young people on board, the ceremony normally takes place by the swimming pool, where people are "shaved" by Father Neptune and there is a lot of horseplay and frivolity and it ends up with the participants being ducked in the pool.'

He paused and took a sip of his drink.

'I don't think our ladies would take very kindly to that,' I said tentatively.

The Captain's eyes grew wide with horror.

'Oh, Mr Durrell, I could not suggest it for one minute. No, no, no,' he said. 'Our ladies are – well – shall we say a little too adult for such behaviour. No, what I have organized is a small banquet. Our chef is really very good when he has the right ingredients and so I have sent him ashore to purchase whatever is needed, fruit, fresh meat and so on. We will of course drink champagne with it. Do you think they will approve of that?'

'My dear Captain, you know they will be enchanted,' I said. 'You have done so much to make this voyage a happy and memorable one for them, and you must know that they are all desperately in love with you.'

The Captain turned the delicate pink of a rose petal.

'Furthermore,' I said, 'in their eyes you can do no wrong and so anything you do will be a fabulous success. The only trouble will be if your wife ever gets to hear about eleven ladies all being in love with you simultaneously.'

The Captain turned an even deeper shade of pink.

'Fortunately, my wife is a very intelligent woman,' he said. 'She has always said to me, "Siegfried, if you fancy another woman that will be all right, but point her out to me so that I may kill her before you start your flirtation."'

'An eminently sensible lady,' I said. 'Let us drink to her.' We did, and then went in to lunch.

After the chilled soup with the remains of some fish floating in it that looked as though it had either been undescribed by science or been rejected by it, the Captain put down his spoon, patted his mouth with his napkin, cleared his throat and leaned forward.

'Mr Durrell, there is something else I would value your opinion on since you are a writer of renown.'

Inwardly I groaned. Was he going to ask me to read and comment on his life story – *Fifty Years at Sea*, or *Typhoons Ahoy?*

'Yes, Captain,' I said, dutifully, 'what is that?'

'I thought that as well as the banquet for our ladies they should have something more lasting to remind them of the event, so I wondered if you, as a writer, would think these suitable.'

He placed on the white table-cloth one of the pieces of paper he had been looking at in the bar, which looked like the sort of archaic parchment which legal documents were written on in the Middle Ages. On each one had been beautifully engraved in the most elegant of copperplate handwriting the name of the ship, its destination, the date on which it was going to cross the line and lastly, with a great flourish of curlicues, the passenger's name. They were most exquisitely executed.

'Captain,' I said in admiration, 'they are wonderful. The ladies will love them. Which talented member of your crew did them?' The Captain blushed again.

'I did them myself,' he said modestly. 'I do a little calligraphy in my spare time.'

'Well, they are truly magnificent and the ladies will be over-whelmed,' I assured him.

'I am glad,' he said, 'I want this to be a happy last voyage for me!'

'Last voyage?' I questioned.

'Yes, when we finish the voyage I am retiring,' he said.

'But you look too young to retire,' I protested.

'Thank you,' he said, giving a courtly little bow, 'but I am at retirement age. I have been at sea since I was sixteen years old and, although I have loved the life, I shall be glad to give it up. Apart from anything else, it has been hard on my dear wife. It is the wives who suffer, particularly if there are no children, for they get lonely.'

'Where are you going to retire to?' I asked.

His face lit up with excitement.

'In the north of my country there is a small but beautiful bay and a very small town called Spitzen,' he said. 'My wife and I purchased a house there some years ago. It is right on the rocks, outside the town on the edge of the bay. It is very beautiful. Do you know I can lie in my bed and watch the seagulls flying past my window? I can hear them calling and the sound of the sea.

41

When we have bad weather the wind hoots round the house like an owl, and the big waves crash like thunder on the shore. It is very exciting.'

'And what will you do?' I asked.

A dreamy expression crossed his pixie face.

'I shall practise my calligraphy,' he said softly, and it was almost as if he were hypnotized by the thought. 'My calligraphy needs attention. I shall paint and I shall play the flute and try to make up to my wife for her years of loneliness. You understand, I do none of these things well – except perhaps the last – but I enjoy trying. They give me pleasure even if badly done, and I think pleasure soothes the mind.'

I raised my glass.

'I drink to your long and happy retirement,' I said.

He gave me one of his quaint, old-fashioned bows.

'Thank you. I hope it will be so. But the most important thing is that it will delight my dear, patient wife,' and he gave me a radiant, unselfish smile.

I went to my cabin for a siesta and was presently apprised of our ladies' return by the pattering of feet and the banging of cabin doors and shrill cries of 'Lucinda, did you have that basket I bought – the red and green one? Oh, thank the Lord, I thought I'd left it in the taxi,' and 'Mabel, I do think you bought too much fruit – those bananas are going to go as rotten as a politician in no time.'

Later, over cocktails, I was shown, in great secrecy, the five sweaters that had been purchased for the Captain. The reason for this plethora of garments was that the ladies fell out over colours once again since (which I should have foreseen) they could not get oatmeal. I was asked to judge which was best and so found myself in a situation that Solomon would not have envied. I picked my way out of this potential minefield by telling the ladies that the Captain had vouchsafed to me that this was his last voyage. Long trembling cries of lamentation filled the saloon as if I was surrounded by a flock of kookaburras deprived of their young. How could this be? He was such an up square bloke. He was so courteous and cultured. He was the sort of foreigner you would entertain in your own home. He was a real gent, one of those real gents what is a real gent if you know what I mean. You would have thought we were discussing the removal of Nelson from the fleet before Trafalgar. I gave everyone more drinks and asked for peace, a hush. I am not quite sure, but I think I said, 'Every cloud has a silver lining.'

Everyone calmed down at the familiar sound of this old platitude and waited expectantly. I said that the Captain and his wife were going to their wonderful house in the north where, in the spring, the flowers were a tapestry of colour and the birds sang like a heavenly choir. But in winter storms lashed the region, lightning fluttered and flashed in the sky like white veins, thunder crashed louder than a million potatoes being dumped on a wooden floor and the waves curled and crashed on the shore like steel blue lions with white frothy manes attacking the land. The ladies were riveted by my excessive imagery. What man, I asked rhetorically, in those circumstances, could do without five pullovers in five different colours? No man could live. Five pullovers for that region were essential for survival. The ladies were entranced. They had, by their united wisdom, saved their hero from hypothermia and so they all had another drink to celebrate.

Two days later the Captain, meticulous as always, had little printed cards placed in each cabin informing us that there would be a special Crossing of the Line dinner party that night. This threw the ladies into a turmoil of excitement. Clothes were taken out, discussed, discarded, reinstated, washed, ironed, discarded once more when some more suitable trophy was suddenly found lurking in the bottom of the suitcase. Make-up flew between cabins like a rainbow. The smell of eleven different scents competing with each other was as fearsome as a forest fire. The squeaks of delight or dismay, the moans of ultimate despair and the cries of joy that echoed from cabin to cabin were as complex and heartwarming as listening to a choir of birds in a forest at dawn. Eventually, every hair carefully washed and rigidly in place, every eyebrow carefully demarcated, each eyelid under a cloak of blue or green, each mouth lipsticked in crimson glory, each bust and each buttock regimented into place, the ladies were ready.

Assembling in the bar, they were greeted by a panoply of ice buckets with champagne lurking in each one. The twittering of delight at this opulence was wonderful.

Then the hero of the hour made his appearance, immaculate in his best uniform, white as any summer cloud, carrying a large cardboard box. When his admiring fans had finished twittering, the Captain opened the box and from it extracted a gardenia for each lady and a red carnation for me. I was thankful I had taken the trouble to unearth my ancient dinner jacket and get the steward to press it into some semblance of decency. The ladies, of course, were overwhelmed. Nobody, not even a straight bloke like what you sometimes come across in Australia, had ever given them gardenias. They kept smelling each other's gardenias and going into rapture over the scent. Then the champagne was poured and there was much girlish giggling and the usual complaints about bubbles up the nose. There was champagne galore, and so we were all very convivial when we went into the dining saloon for the banquet.

They had really done us proud. The white damask cloth had been decorated with fresh flowers and from somewhere they had unearthed enough cut glasses for the wine. The first course was a delicious pâté. This was followed by some superb smoked salmon rolled up with a filling of cream, horseradish and dill. Then came chicken, done in a delicate wine sauce, with a delicious variety of vegetables to accompany it and those wonderful potato puffs called, appropriately enough, Perflutters. This was followed by cheese and then an enormous Bombe Surprise was brought in to excited cries of wonderment and delight. When this had been demolished and coffee was served, the Captain stood up and made a speech

'Ladies, Mr Durrell,' he said, giving one of his old-fashioned, bird-like bows to us all. 'This is a special occasion. I know that Mr Durrell who travels a great deal has crossed the line many times. But I know it is the first time you ladies have, and so your crossing from one side of the world to the other is an important moment. So we must celebrate it.'

He walked over to the big sideboard that lined one side of the dining saloon and carefully picked up the scrolls he had laboured over. He carried them to the table and piled them by his plate.

'So,' he continued, 'I have prepared here, for each one of you, a document which states that you have crossed the line, and that you have crossed it on my ship. I hope you will like them.'

There was an excited murmur from his mesmerized audience.

'So ladies,' he said, raising his wine glass, 'may I drink to you all, your health and happiness and thank you for making my last voyage such a pleasure.'

Smiling, he raised his glass. Then the glass flew from his hand, scattering gouts of wine on the table-cloth, and he dropped dead.

To say we were stunned would be an understatement. I had been watching his charming face as he made his little speech and his eyes had just suddenly glazed over. There was no wince as of great pain. The only indication there was anything wrong with him was the spilt wine and the fact that he fell over sideways, stiff as a log of wood, and crashed on to the floor at the feet of his Chief Officer and the purser, who were standing to one side, ready to give out the scrolls. Both of them, dumbfounded, stood there like statues. I turned to Mrs Malrepose, sitting on my right, by far the most down to earth and practical of the ladies.

'Get everyone to the bar. We'll attend to the Captain,' I said.

She gave me an anguished look, but nodded. I got round the table with all speed. The Chief Officer and the purser were still standing there with their dead Captain at their feet as though they were on parade.

'Loosen his collar,' I said. The Chief Officer gave a start, as if waking suddenly. The Captain was wearing an old-fashioned starched collar with a gold stud, so it was some seconds before it became free. There was no throb from the vein in his neck, nor was there any flutter under the fragile basketwork of his ribs. I stood up.

'He's dead,' I said, somewhat unnecessarily.

The Chief Officer looked at me.

'What do we do?' he asked, a man regimented to take orders and not control.

'Look,' I said, exasperated, 'if a captain on a British merchant ship drops dead, I believe that the chief officer becomes captain. So you're now captain.'

He stared at me, his eyes expressionless.

'But what do we do?' he asked.

'For God's sake,' I said angrily, 'you're captain, so you tell us what to do.'

'What would you suggest?' he asked.

I looked at him.

'Firstly,' I said, 'I would get your poor ex-captain up off the floor and carried to his cabin. Next, I would strip him and wash him and lay him out decently. Then I suppose you have to get in touch with Head Office and tell them what's happened. Meanwhile, I will deal with the ladies.'

'Yes, sir,' he said, happy now that someone was giving orders.

'Oh, and if we have to bury him at sea, try and do it at night, otherwise we will have the ladies in a hellish state of melancholy.'

'Yes, sir,' he said. 'I will arrange that.'

I went into the saloon, where I was met by tears and anxious enquiries after their hero's health.

'Ladies, I have bad news, I'm afraid,' I said. 'Our beloved Captain is no longer with us. However . . .'

But my words were drowned by a burst of lamentation that was overwhelming. They clasped each other, tears rocketing down their cheeks, their sobs heartrending. They were as deeply shocked and affected as if it had been one of their own intimate circle who had died. I had heard of people wringing their hands, but never seen it. This is what they all did. They gave vent to their grief in the complete way that Greeks do, an uninhibited display of their love for the Captain. I signalled the barman, who looked as stunned as we all felt.

'Brandies for everyone,' I whispered to him, 'and big ones.'

When each lady was tremblingly clasping a goblet half full of brandy, half full of tears, I made a speech.

'Ladies,' I said, 'I would like you all to listen to me for a moment.' I felt like Ronald Reagan trying to play Shakespeare.

Obediently as children, they turned their tear-besmudged faces to me, green and blue eye-shadow awry, eyelashes glued together by tears – and the careful make-up eroded.

'Our beloved Captain has been taken from us.' I said. 'He was a dear, kind man and we shall miss him terribly. Now I want you to raise your glasses and drink to a wonderful man, but as you do so I want you to remember three things. Firstly, he would be the last one to want us to be unhappy, for as you all know he did his best to *make* us happy.'

There was a loud sob from Mrs Meadowsweet, which was immediately shushed by the other ladies, I was glad to see.

'Secondly,' I said, 'I was watching him carefully and I can assure you he died without pain. Isn't that what we would all like for our nearest and dearest and, indeed, for ourselves when the time comes?'

There was a murmuration of agreement.

'The third thing is this,' I continued. 'When you were all ashore, I had lunch with the Captain and while we talked he confessed to me that having you ladies on board had made his last voyage wonderfully memorable to him. In fact, he confirmed that, if asked, he would have a difficult time in saying which of you ladies he loved the best.'

There was a faint rustle of satisfaction and pride.

'So let us drink to our friend the Captain, whom we will never forget.'

'Never!' said the ladies stalwartly.

We all drank and I signalled the barman for another round. Presently, the ladies, very unsober, but not nearly as hysterical, drifted off to their cabins. I was just about to do the same when the Chief Officer materialized at my elbow. He was the last person I wanted to see. While dealing with the ladies, I also had my own private grief for the Captain to contend with.

'I have done as you suggested, sir,' he said.

'Good,' I said curtly, 'although why you are reporting to me I cannot think. *You're* the bloody captain now.'

'Yes, sir,' he said, 'and his widow wants his body to be buried at his home town.'

'Well?' I said. 'Take him there.'

'Yes, sir,' he said and paused, his eyes as expressionless as ever. Then he said, 'I am sorry this happened. I liked the Captain.'

'Me too,' I said tiredly. 'He was a nice, kind, gentle man and they are as rare as unicorns.'

'As what, sir?' he asked.

'Never mind, I'm going to bed. Good night.'

By the morning, the ladies had recovered to a certain extent. There was the odd snuffle, the odd tear, but the Captain was referred to in the past tense as his many virtues were extolled. As we progressed over the miles and miles of blue and empty water – empty that is except for the groups of dolphin, exuberant as children let out of school, who appeared now and then and did a ballet round the ship – the heat became intense. Mrs Meadowsweet and Mrs Farthingale got nasty cases of sunburn, through falling asleep on the deck. Mrs Malrepose suffered from heatstroke and had to be put to bed in a darkened cabin with cold compresses, but apart from that nothing of moment happened. Having been brought up in the sun I revelled in it and I worked hard at building up a tan that would be everybody's envy. But eventually the blistering heat became too much for me and I retired to my cabin. It was there, in the cool dimness, that the former Chief Officer came to see me.

'I am sorry to worry you, sir,' he said, 'but I have a problem with the Captain.'

I was both startled and confused as I had become used to thinking of him as the captain.

'You mean you have a problem with our ex-captain?' I asked.

'Yes, sir,' he said, and he shifted rather uneasily from foot to foot and then blurted out, 'he is starting to be offensive.'

I could not think what he was talking about.

'How do you mean, offensive?' I asked in puzzlement. 'He's dead!' He looked around the small cabin furtively, making sure we had no eavesdroppers.

'He is starting to – to – to – well, he is starting *smelling*,' he said in a hushed voice, as one uttering a blasphemy.

I was horrified.

'D'you mean to say that in *this* heat you've still got his corpse in his *cabin*?' I asked incredulously.

'Yes, sir, that is where you told us to put him,' he said aggrievedly.

'But in this heat, man, it's ridiculous. Why didn't you put him in a fridge?'

He looked startled.

'You mean with the food?' he said.

'No, but your refrigeration area is huge. Surely there is a corner where you can put him?'

'I will go and see,' he said, and went off.

Presently he was back again.

'I have found a place, sir, in the meat locker. I have put him in there,' he reported.

'Good,' I said, with a sudden macabre vision of my sweet Captain lying among the swinging sides of beef and lamb. 'Now, for heaven's sake, the ladies must not know this on any account, you understand?'

'Yes, sir,' he said firmly. 'They will not know.'

So the voyage continued and, apart from a little bad weather – nothing more than a gentle rolling swell, but it had the ladies confined to their cabins and the smell of eau de Cologne was overwhelming – everything went smoothly enough. The ladies' spirits recovered and they even started to accept the Chief Officer as captain, complimenting him and the purser on the wonderful salads, the multi-coloured ice creams and the quality of the lamb chops and steaks. I wondered what they would have said if they had found out that their hero, the Captain, was down there in the frozen darkness among the foodstuffs they were consuming. It was best not to contemplate such a horrific catastrophe.

49

It was the night before we docked. The ladies were all busy packing and the sounds of this laborious process echoed up and down from cabin to cabin. There was the usual banging of doors and pattering feet. Cries of 'Lucinda, have you got my green I lent you?', 'Mabel, can you come and sit on my suitcase? I don't know why it is, but suitcases always seem to bite off more than they can chew', and 'Edna, I swear to you, darling, if you pack that whisky in the bottom of your case, you'll smell like a refugee from Alcoholics Anonymous when we land.'

I made my way to the bar for a pre-dinner drink. It was empty except for the Chief Officer who was imbibing a brandy. The bottle stood on the bar in front of him and I saw that he had been making very steady inroads on its contents.

'Good evening,' I said.

He straightened up and stared at me. I suspected that he was fairly drunk, but it was difficult to tell from his curious expressionless eyes.

'Good evening, sir,' he said. Then after a pause he gestured at the bottle. 'You will have a drink?'

'Thank you,' I said and, since the barman appeared to have become extinct, I got myself a glass from behind the bar and poured myself a drink from his bottle. Silence fell over the two of us like a muffling fog. I let it last for a minute or two and then decided to dispel it.

'Well,' I said jovially, 'I expect you're glad the voyage is over. Now you'll be able to have a little rest at home. Whereabouts do you live?'

He looked at me unhearingly.

'I am having trouble with the Captain,' he said.

I felt a preliminary tingle of apprehension crawl up my spine. 'What sort of trouble?' I asked.

'It is my fault, I should have looked,' he said.

'What *sort* of trouble?' I repeated.

'If I had looked it would not have happened,' he said, and poured himself a formidable whack of brandy.

'What would not have happened?' I asked.

He drank deeply and was silent for a moment.

'You remember when we took the Captain from his cabin and put him – put him – put him downstairs?'

'Yes.'

'He was still soft, you understand? Just after that we have bad weather and the ladies are sick.' He shrugged. 'Not bad weather for *us*, but for them, yes. A long rolling swell. It makes people sick.' He took another drink.

'And,' he continued, 'it made the Captain move.'

'Move?' I said, startled. 'What do you mean?'

'We laid him flat but with the movement of the ship he rolled and his legs came up.'

He lifted one of his bent legs to waist height and slapped his thigh.

'It was my fault. I did not check. You see he was still warm and so he froze like that, in that position.'

He paused and drank again.

'The carpenter had made the coffin, so this evening we went down to put the Captain in it, how you say in English? So he is all shipshape and Bristol fashion ready for his wife.'

I would not have put it quite like that, but it was not a moment for a lesson in English colloquialisms. I was beginning to feel rather sick.

'We tried everything,' he said, 'everything. I got the two strongest men on the ship, but they could not straighten his legs. It was impossible. And we had to have him in the coffin tonight. The paper work, you know? We had not time to – you know – thaw him.'

He flooded a large, golden pool of brandy into his glass and gulped it down.

'So I broke his legs with a mallet,' he said, and turned and left the bar, weaving slightly from side to side.

I shivered and poured myself a brandy of equal size to the one the Chief Officer had just downed. I stood for a moment remembering the Captain, his charm, his gallantry with the ladies, his gentleness, but above all I remembered how he was going to draw, play his flute, and lie in bed with his beloved wife and watch the seagulls go past their bedroom window. I decided that retirement was something you should take a little bit of every day, like a tonic, for you never knew what awaited you around the corner.

I also decided that I didn't want any dinner.

Marrying Off Mother

That summer in Corfu was a particularly good one. The night skies were a heavy velvety blue with, apparently, more stars than ever before, like a crop of tiny burnished mushrooms glinting in the vast blue meadow. The moon seemed twice as large as normal, starting – as we turned towards her and she lifted herself into the night sky – as orange as a tangerine and then undergoing colour changes from apricot to daffodil yellow before hatching out into a miraculous white, as white as a bride's gown, the light from which cast pools of bright silver among the hunched and twisted olives. Excited by the warmth and beauty of these nights, the fireflies would attempt to emulate and outdo the stars and so formed their own glittering, throbbing conglomerations among the trees where the Scops owls chimed like mournful little bells. At dawn the eastern sky would have a blood red line drawn across, the sword of the approaching sun. This would change to canary yellow, then lilac, and finally as the sun made his splendid appearance over the horizon the sky would suddenly turn as blue as flax and the stars would be extinguished as one blows out candles after a gigantic ball.

I used to wake just before the sun's rim flooded our world with light and contemplate my room and its contents. The room was large with two big windows and slatted shutters that used to make friendly musical noises when touched by the slightest wind. In winter it was an orchestra. The floor was a wooden one of plain scrubbed boards that creaked and grumbled, in one corner of which were two elderly blankets and a pillow on which my three dogs, Roger, Widdle and Puke, slept in a snoring, twitching huddle. The other accoutrements of a normal bedroom were lacking. True, there was a cupboard, allegedly for hanging up my clothes, but in reality most of its space was taken up with more sensible things, like my various forked sticks for catching snakes, my different nets for catching insects, for delving into ponds and ditches and stouter ones for marine captures, as well as fishing rods and useful poles with three large hooks on the end for pulling pond- or seaweed within reach and thus facilitating the capture of those creatures that dwelt in their green, feathery grottoes.

There was, of course, a table, but this was piled high with my nature notes, books, test-tubes full of specimens and, on this particular day, I recall, the semi-dissected corpse of a hedgehog I had found which, even by my broad-minded standards, was starting to make its presence felt. Round the room there were shelves containing aquariums and glass-fronted cages in which crouched bulbous-eyed mantids who regarded you malevolently, tree frogs like green velvet, geckos with stomach skin so fine you could see their internal organs through it, newts in their watery world and baby terrapins the size of walnuts. Presiding over all this on top of the window pelmet was Ulysses, my Scops owl, looking like a slim statue carved from ash-grey wood streaked with Maltese crosses in black, his eyes like oriental slits against the intrusive sunlight.

In the garden below I could hear the yapping of my seagull Alecko calling for fish and the wicked witch's cackle of my two magpies. The half-closed shutters were making a pattern of tiger stripes across the bare boards. The air was hot even at that hour. The sheets were hot and, even though I slept naked and it was only just past dawn, I could feel areas of sweat on my body. I got out of bed and padded across to open the shutters and a blinding flood of dandelion-coloured sunlight poured into the room. The dogs stretched, yawned, clippered themselves briefly with their front teeth to disturb a brood of worrying fleas and stood up wagging their tails. Having ascertained that Sally, my donkey, was still tethered to the almond tree where I had left her the evening before, and that no dastardly member of the peasantry had stolen her, I got dressed. This was a simple process. Slip on shorts and a cobweb linen shirt, slide feet into well worn sandals and I was ready to face what the day might bring. The first hurdle to overcome was having breakfast with my family and being as unobtrusive as possible in case my elder brother Larry had smelt the hedgehog. His olfactory senses were far too well developed for a brother to possess, in my opinion. We had breakfast in the little sunken garden that ran along and below our broad, flagged veranda, cloaked in vine. The garden was very Victorian looking, with small flowerbeds in squares, rounds, triangles or stars, carefully rimmed with white stone. In each bed stood a small tangerine tree, whose scent, when the sun shone on them, was almost overpowering. In the beds at their feet grew nice old-fashioned flowers, forget-me-nots, pinks, lavender, sweet-william, night-scented stock, tobacco plants and lilies of the valley. It was a sort of Piccadilly Circus for the local insects and so was a favourite hunting ground of mine, for there was everything from butterflies to antlions, lacewing flies to rose beetles, great fat burring bumble bees to tiny wasps.

The table was set in the shade of the tangerine trees, and round it arranging plates and knives would hobble Lugaretzia, our maid, groaning gently to herself. She was a professional hypochondriac and was always cherishing and cosseting six or seven ailments at any time and would, if you were not careful, give you vivid and sometimes disgusting descriptions of what the interior of her stomach was doing, or how her varicose veins throbbed like a savage tribe's tom-toms when on the warpath.

This day I noted with satisfaction that we were having scrambled eggs. Mother used to simmer chopped onions until they were transparent and then add the beaten eggs that had yolks as brilliant as the sun and came from our own family of chickens. One day my sister Margo, in a philanthropic mood, let all the chickens out of their pen for a walk. They found a patch of wild garlic and feasted on it, with the result that the omelettes for breakfast the next morning were thoroughly impregnated. My brother Leslie complained that it was like eating the upholstery out of a Greek bus.

Scrambled eggs were really something to start the day on. I generally had two helpings and then followed this up with four or five huge slices of brown toast covered with a thick coating of honey from our own hives. Lest I be thought greedy, let me hasten to say that eating this much toast and honey was much like following a natural history lesson or an archaeological dig. The hives were in the charge of Lugaretzia's husband, a fragile-looking man who seemed to have the cares of the world on his shoulders, as, indeed, he had, as anyone spending ten minutes in his wife's company would readily perceive. Whenever he deprived our five hives of bees of their carefully garnered provender he was always stung so severely that he would have to spend several days in bed. As he was being stung, however, he inevitably dropped several honey-combs on the ground, where they became a magnificent sticky trap for any insect that happened to be around. In spite of Mother's desperate attempts to strain the honey before it came to table, there was always a small and interesting zoological collection lurking there. So spreading the musky, brown-gold delicacy on your bread was like spreading out liquid amber in which you might find almost anything from tiny moths and caterpillars to beetles and small centipedes. Once, to my delight, I found a species of earwig that was unknown to me. So breakfast was always a biologically interesting meal. The rest of my family, who, to my chagrin, remained defiantly unzoological, did not share my pleasure at the rich bounty the honey provided.

It was at breakfast that we read our mail, if any, which arrived once a week. I never got any letters, but used to make up for it by receiving the *Animal and Zoo Magazine*, together with other erudite literature containing *The Adventures of Black Beauty*, *Rin-tin-tin* and similar zoological heroes. As we ate and read, each one of us would read out titbits from letters or magazines for the rest of the family who would remain totally oblivious.

'Murdoch is publishing his life story,' Larry would snort. 'How young do we have to be before inflicting autobiographies on an unsuspecting public? He can't be more than twenty-four. Can I have some more tea?'

'There's a rhinoceros been born at a zoo in Switzerland,' I would inform my family jubilantly.

'Really, dear? How nice for them,' my mother would say, busy with her seed catalogue.

'They say organdie is coming back into fashion *and* puffed sleeves,' Margo would vouchsafe, 'and about time too, in my opinion.'

'Yes, dear,' Mother would say. 'I'm sure that zinnias would do here. In that bed behind the beehives. It gets a lot of warmth.'

'I bet my collection of flintlocks would fetch a fortune in England. They're selling awful-looking ones at fantastic prices,' Leslie would inform an unlistening audience, browsing through his gun catalogue. 'That one I got for twenty drachs the other day, I expect in London it would fetch pounds.'

However, although apparently uncaringly sunk each in our own mail, strangely the family's antennae would be out and quivering, discarding most of what was said but transforming us into an indignant mob should someone vouchsafe something displeasing. On this particular morning Larry started the whole thing, or to be more honest he lit the fuse that led to the keg of powder.

'Oh, splendid,' he said, 'I'm so glad, Antoine de Vere is coming to stay.'

Mother peered at him over her glasses.

'Now, look here, Larry,' she said, 'we've just got rid of one lot of your friends. I'm not having another lot. It's too much. It's too exhausting, what with preparing the food and Lugaretzia's legs and everything.'

Larry gave her a pained look.

'I'm not asking you to cook Lugaretzia's legs for Antoine,' he said. 'I am sure they would be most unsavoury if what she tells me about them is to be believed.'

'Larry, don't be so disgusting,' said Margo primly.

'I didn't say anything about cooking Lugaretzia's legs,' said

57

Mother, flustered. 'Apart from anything else, she's got varicose veins.'

'I'm sure in New Guinea they would be considered a delicacy. They probably eat them like spaghetti,' said Larry. 'But Antoine has a very cultured palate, and I don't think he'd care for them, even disguised in breadcrumbs.'

'I'm not talking about Lugaretzia's veins,' said my mother indignantly.

'Well, *you* were the one who brought them up,' said Larry. 'I merely suggested a disguise of breadcrumbs to make them seem more *haute cuisine*.'

'Larry, you do make me angry sometimes,' said my mother, 'and don't go about telling people about Lugaretzia's legs as if they were something I kept in the larder.'

'Who is this De Vere whatnot, anyway?' asked Leslie. 'Another one of those wet pansies, I suppose?'

'Don't you *know* who he is?' asked Margo, wide-eyed. 'Why, he's a great film actor. He's made films in Hollywood. He almost made a film with Jean Harlow. He's making one in England now. He's dark – and – and – and he's dark and he's . . .'

'Dark?' suggested Leslie.

'Handsome,' said Margo. 'At least, *some* people might call him handsome I don't think he is. I think he's too old, if you ask me. He must be thirty. I mean, I wouldn't be interested in a handsome film star if he was that old, would you?'

'I wouldn't be interested in him if he was handsome, a film star, old and a male,' said Leslie with finality.

'When you two have finished this character assassination of my friend . . .' Larry began.

'Now, don't quarrel, dears,' said Mother. 'Really, you children do quarrel about the stupidest things. Now, the Beer man, whatever he's called. Can't you put him off, Larry? It's been a very hectic summer with so many people coming to stay and it's very tiring and then there's the food . . .'

'You mean you're frightened that Lugaretzia's legs won't go round?' asked Larry.

Mother gave him her most ferocious glare, a glare that might just possibly have given a moment of unease to a fledgling sparrow.

'Now, don't go on about Lugaretzia's veins, Larry, or I will get seriously annoyed,' she said. It was her favourite threat and we could never work out what the difference was between being annoyed and being seriously annoyed. Mother, presumably, had it fixed in her mind that there were different grades of annoyance, as there were different colours in a rainbow.

'Anyway, I can't put him off, even if I wanted to,' said Larry, 'this letter's dated the twelfth, so he's probably halfway here. I should think he will arrive on the Athens boat next week or the week after. So I should pop those veins into a cauldron and get them simmering if I were you. I have no doubt that Gerry can supply some other ingredients like the odd toad. He has something decaying gently in his room at the moment, so my nose tells me.'

I was dismayed. He had smelt the hedgehog, and I'd only got as far as the lungs in my dissection. This was the disadvantage of having an elder brother occupying the bedroom next to yours.

'Well,' said Mother, conceding defeat, 'if there's only one of him, I suppose we can cope.'

'There was only one of him when we last met,' said my brother. 'We shall only know if, by some strange alchemy, he has been transformed into twins when he arrives. I should get Lugaretzia to make up two beds, just in case.'

'Do you know what he eats?' Mother asked, obviously working out menus in her head.

'Food,' said Larry, succinctly.

'You do make me cross,' said Mother. Silence reigned, while everyone concentrated on his or her letter or magazine. Magically, time drifted by as it had a habit of doing in Corfu.

'I wonder whether passion flowers would look nice on that east wall,' said Mother, looking up from her seed catalogue. 'They are so pretty. I can imagine the east wall just covered with passion flowers, can't you?'

'We could do with a bit of passion around here,' said Larry. 'Just recently, the place has been as chaste as a nunnery.'

'I don't see what passion flowers have got to do with nuns,' said Mother.

Larry sighed and gathered up his mail.

'Why don't you get married again?' he suggested. 'You've been looking awfully wilted lately, rather like an overworked nun.'

'Indeed I haven't,' said Mother indignantly.

'You're looking sort of shrewish and spinsterish,' said Larry, 'rather like Lugaretzia on a good day. And all this mooning about passion flowers. It's very Freudian. Obviously what you want is a dollop of romance in your life. Get married again.'

'What rubbish you talk, Larry,' said my mother, bridling. 'Get married again! What nonsense! Your father would never allow it.'

'Dad's been dead nearly twelve years. I think his objection could be overruled, don't you? Get married again and make us all legitimate.'

'Larry, stop talking like that in front of Gerry,' said my mother, getting more and more flustered. 'You're being perfectly ridiculous. You're as legitimate as I am.'

'And you're being hard-hearted and callous, allowing your selfish feelings to crush the natural instincts of your family,' Larry said. 'How can we boys develop a good, healthy Oedipus complex without a father to hate? How can Margo hate you properly if she doesn't have a father to fall in love with? You're letting us grow into monsters of depravity. How can we flourish and become like other people if we don't have a step-father to loathe and despise? It's your duty as a mother to marry again. It would be the making of you as a woman. As it is you're just dwindling away and becoming a sour old faggot. Get romance while you can still hobble about after the opposite sex and bring a little joy into your children's lives and a bit of passion into your own.'

'Larry, I'm not going to sit here and listen to this nonsense. Marry again, indeed. In any case, who would I marry?' said Mother, falling into the trap.

'Well, you were saying how good-looking that boy who runs the fish stall at Garitza is, the other day,' Larry pointed out.

'Are you *mad*?' asked Mother. 'He's only about eighteen.'

'What does age matter when passion is involved?' Larry asked. 'They say Catherine the Great had fifteen-year-old lovers when she was well into her seventies.'

'Larry, don't be disgusting,' said Mother, 'and don't say things like that in front of Gerry. I'm not going to listen to any more of your twaddle. I'm going to look at Lugaretzia.'

'Well, take my word for it, looking at Lugaretzia would pale into insignificance if you had the choice between her and the fish-monger at Garitza,' warned Larry.

Mother gave him one of her glares and went off to the kitchen. There was a pause as we all reflected.

'You know, Larry, I think for once you're right,' said Margo. 'Mother has been looking down in the dumps recently. She's got a sort of left-on-the-shelf air about her. I think it's unhealthy. She needs to be taken out of herself.'

'Yes,' said Leslie. 'I personally think it's too much contact with Lugaretzia. These things are catching.'

'You mean varicose veins are catching?' asked Margo, looking down with alarm at her legs.

'No, no,' said Leslie, irritably, 'I mean all this moaning and depression.'

'I agree,' said Larry, 'ten minutes with Lugaretzia is like having a night out with Boris Karloff and the Hunchback of Nôtre-Dame. There's no doubt about it, we must try to think of a way of saving Mother for posterity. After all, under our guidance she was doing so well up until now. I will give my mind to it.'

With that ominous pronouncement he went off to his room and the rest of us dispersed about our various affairs and forgot about our mother's sad lack of a soul mate.

At lunchtime, when we were all sitting on the veranda, wondering if we would melt before Mother and Lugaretzia managed to get food to us, Spiro arrived in his ancient Dodge piled high with multifarious goodies for the larder, ranging from water melons to tomatoes, a vast quantity of bread, whose mouth-watering crusts were peeling off the loaves as cork bark peels from a cork tree. There were also three huge coffin-shaped blocks of ice wrapped in sacking for our ice box, Mother's pride and joy, designed by her and of enormous proportions.

Spiro had entered our lives on our arrival in Corfu as a taxi driver and within hours had transformed himself into our guide, mentor and friend. His curious command of the English language – learnt during a sojourn in Chicago – absolved Mother of the insoluble problems of trying to master the Greek tongue. His adoration of her was complete and selfless, as his often repeated phrase 'Gollys, if I hads a mother like yours I'd go down on my knees and kisses her feets every morning' bore witness. He was a short, barrel-shaped man with massive dark eyebrows and those black, brooding, unreadable eyes that only Greeks appear to possess, fixed in a brown face like a benevolent gargoyle. Now he lumbered on to the veranda and went through the litany we did not want but which seemed to give him pleasure.

'Good morning, Missy Margo. Good morning, Mr Larry. Good morning, Mr Leslies. Good morning, Master Gerrys,' he intoned and like a well-trained choir we would all say, 'Good morning, Spiro,' in unison. When this ritual was over, Larry took a thoughtful sip of his post-prandial ouzo.

'Spiro, we have a problem,' he confessed. It was like saying 'walkies' to a bull mastiff. Spiro stiffened and his eyes narrowed.

'You tells me, Mr Larrys,' he said, in a voice which was so deep and rich it sounded like the birth cries of Krakatoa. 'I'll fixes it.'

'It may be difficult,' Larry admitted.

'Don'ts you worrys, I'll fixes it,' said Spiro with all the conviction of one who knows everyone on the island and who could make anyone do anything.

'Well,' said Larry, 'it's about my mother.'

Spiro's face took on a reddish tinge and he took a step forward. 'What's the matters with yours mothers?' he said in alarm, his plurals coming thick and fast.

'Well, she wants to get married again,' said Larry, calmly lighting a cigarette. We were all breathless. Of all the audacious things Larry had ever perpetrated, this had to be the most formidable and far reaching.

Spiro stood immobile, staring at my brother.

'Yours mothers wants to gets marrieds *again*?' he said hoarsely, in an incredulous voice. 'Tells me who this man is and I'll fix him, Mr Larrys. Don'ts you worrys.'

'How would you fix him?' asked Leslie with interest, who, with his enormous collection of guns and his hunting forays, tended to let his mind travel along lines of death and destruction rather than those of sweetness and humanitarianism.

'Likes they teaches me in Chicago,' said Spiro, scowling. 'Cement boots.'

'Cement boots?' asked Margo, her attention attracted now that the conversation had apparently turned to fashion. 'What on earth are those?'

'Well, you get this bastard – if you'll excuses the words, Missy Margo – and you stick his feet in a couple of buckets of cement. When it gets hard you take him out in a caique and drop him overboard,' Spiro explained.

'But you couldn't do that!' Margo exclaimed. 'He wouldn't be able to swim. He'd drown.'

'That's the idea,' Larry explained patiently.

'I think you're all perfectly horrible,' said Margo. 'It's disgusting. It's murder, that's what it is, just pure murder. And, anyway, I'm not having *my* step-father going about in cement gumboots or whatever they are. I mean, if he drowned, we would all be orphans.'

'No, there's Mother,' said Leslie.

Margo's eyes widened in horror.

'You're not putting any cement near Mother,' she said. 'I warn you, I shall go straight to the police.'

'Oh, Margo, for heaven's sake, shut up,' said Larry. 'Nobody's saying anything about drowning Mother. In any case, we can't carry out Spiro's ingenious little experiment unless we have a candidate, and this is what we lack. You see, Spiro, Mother has merely expressed a wish to – as it were – have another round with romance. She has not yet decided on any particular man.'

'So when she decides, Mr Larrys, you lets me knows and me and Theodorakis, we gives him the cement boots, OK?'

'But I thought we were trying to *help* Mother to get married again?' said Margo. 'I mean, if Spiro goes and puts cement round the legs of every man she looks at, he'll be a mass murderer, like Rasputin the Ripper, and we'll never get Mother married off.'

'Yes, Spiro, just keep an eye out, will you? Don't do anything drastic but keep us informed,' said Larry, 'and above all, not a word to Mother. She's rather sensitive about this subject.'

'My lips are seals,' said Spiro.

For several days we forgot our mother's mateless existence, for there were many things to do. Several local villages had wonderful fiestas which we always attended. Fleets of donkeys were tethered to trees (for the relatives of the villagers had come from far away, some as far as six miles). The smoke drifting through the olive trees was like a heavy perfume of burning charcoal, roasting lamb and the piquancy of garlic. The wine, red as the blood from a dragon's slaughtering, whispered into the glasses in a purring, conspiratorial way that was so warm and friendly that it nudged you to have some more. The dances were gay, with much leaping in the air and leg-slapping. At the first fiesta, Leslie tried to jump over a bonfire that looked like the internal organs of Vesuvius. He failed to make it and before eager hands pulled him out, his nether regions were burnt quite nastily. He had to sit on an inflatable rubber cushion for a day or two.

It was during one of these fiestas that Larry steered through the merrymaking throng a small man in an immaculate white suit, wearing a cravat of crimson and gold silk and an exquisite panama hat. The shoes on his tiny feet were as burnished as a beetle.

'Mother,' said Larry. 'I have brought over somebody most interesting who is dying to meet you. This is Professor Euripides Androtheomatacottopolous.'

'It is so nice to meet you,' said Mother nervously.

'I am enchanted, Madame Durrell,' said the professor, pressing the back of her hand into the well-clipped beard and moustache that concealed the bottom part of his face like a snowfall.

'The professor is not only a gourmet of renown, but a ruthless exponent of the Culinary arts.'

'Ah, my boy, you exaggerate,' said the professor. 'I am sure my humble efforts in the kitchen would pale into insignificance when compared to the positively Roman banquets that your mother presides over, so I am told.'

Mother always had difficulty in distinguishing between a Roman banquet and a Roman orgy. She had it firmly fixed in her mind that the two were synonymous, implying a great deal of food with half-naked men and women doing things to each other between the soup and the sweet course which were better kept for the privacy of the bedroom.

'Now,' said the professor, sitting down beside her. 'I want you to tell me all you know about the local herbs. Is it true they do not use lavender here?'

This was of course, as Larry well knew, one of Mother's favourite subjects and, seeing that the professor was keenly interested and knowledgeable, she launched herself into a gastronomic diatribe.

Later, when the last mouthful of crisp sheep skin and pink flesh had been eaten, when the last bottle had been emptied and the pulsating heart of each bonfire stamped out, we filed into the faithful Dodge and went home.

'I had *such* an interesting talk with Professor Andro—, Andro—, Andro—, oh, I can't think why the Greeks have such unpronounceable names,' she said crossly, and then leant forward and touched Spiro's shoulder. 'Of course, I don't mean *you*, Spiro, you can't help being called Hak—, Haki—'

'Hakiopolous,' said Spiro.

'Yes. But this professor's name goes on and on forever, like a caterpillar. Still, I suppose it's better than being called Smith or Jones,' Mother sighed.

'Was he interesting about cooking, in spite of his name?' asked Larry.

'Oh, he was fascinating,' said Mother. 'I've invited him to dinner tomorrow night.'

'Good,' said Larry. 'I hope you've got a chaperone.'

'What on earth are you talking about?' asked Mother.

'Well, it's your first date, you've got to do it properly.'

'Larry, don't be so foolish,' said Mother with great dignity, and silence reigned in the car until we reached home.

'Do you think he's the right sort of person to introduce Mother to?' asked Margo worriedly the next day, while Mother was in the kitchen preparing delicacies for the professor's visit.

'Why not?' asked Larry.

'Well, he's so old for one thing. He must be at least fifty,' Margo pointed out.

'Prime of life,' said Larry, airily. 'Men have been known to sire children in their mid-eighties.'

'I don't know why you always have to drag sex in,' Margo complained. 'And anyway, he's a Greek. She can't marry a Greek.'

'Why not?' asked Larry. 'Greeks marry Greeks all the time.'

'But that's different,' said Margo, 'that's their affair. But Mother's British.'

'I agree with Larry,' said Leslie, unexpectedly. 'He's apparently very well off, with two houses in Athens and one in Crete. I don't see that it matters if he's a Greek. He can't help it and anyway, we know some jolly nice Greeks – look at Spiro.'

'She can't marry Spiro, he's married,' said Margo in flustered tones.

'I don't mean *marry* Spiro, I just mean he's a nice Greek.'

'Well, anyway, I don't agree with mixed marriages,' said Margo, 'that's the way you get doubloons.'

'Quadroons,' said Larry.

'Well, whatever they're called,' said Margo, 'I don't want Mother to have one, and I don't want a step-father whose name nobody can pronounce.'

'We'll be on Christian name terms by then,' Larry pointed out.

'What's his Christian name?' asked Margo suspiciously.

'Euripides,' Larry replied. 'You can call him Rip for short.'

To say that the professor made a bad impression that evening would be understating the case. As the horse-drawn carachino that brought him clopped and jingled its way up our long twisting drive through the olive groves we could hear him before we could see him. He was singing a very beautiful Greek love song. Unfortunately, no one had ever told him that he was completely tone deaf, or if they had he did not believe them. He sang lustily and so made up for what he lacked in quality by quantity. We all went out on to the veranda to greet him and, as the carachino came to a halt at our front steps, it became immediately apparent that the professor had partaken of the grape in unwise measure. He fell out of the carachino on to the steps, with the unfortunate result that he broke the three bottles of wine and the jar of home-made chutney he had brought for Mother. The front of his elegant pale grey suit was drenched in wine, so that he looked rather like the miraculous survivor of a very nasty car accident.

'He is drunk,' said the carachino driver, in case this had escaped our notice.

'He's as pooped as an owl,' said Leslie.

'Two owls,' said Larry.

'It's disgusting,' said Margo. 'Mother can't marry a Greek drunkard. Dad would never have approved.'

'Marry *him*? What are you talking about?' asked Mother.

'Just thought he'd bring a bit of romance into your life,' Larry explained, 'I told you we needed a step-father.'

'Marry him,' exclaimed Mother, horrified. 'I wouldn't be seen dead with him. What on earth are you children thinking about?'

'There you are,' said Margo triumphantly, 'I told you she wouldn't want a Greek.'

The professor had taken off his wine-stained Homburg, bowed to Mother and then fallen asleep on the front steps.

'Larry, Leslie, you're making me seriously annoyed,' said Mother. 'Pick up that drunken fool, put him back in the carachino and tell the driver to take him back where he found him, and I never want to see him again.'

'I think you're being thoroughly unromantic,' said Larry. 'How can we get you married again if you adopt this anti-social attitude? The chap's only had a few drinks.'

'And let's have less of this stupid talk about my being married again,' said Mother firmly. '*I'll* tell you when I want to get married and to whom, if ever.'

'We were only trying to help,' said Leslie, aggrieved.

'Well you can help me by getting that drunken idiot out of here,' said Mother, and she strutted back into the villa.

Dinner that night was – conversationally speaking – chilly, but delicious. The professor did not know what he had missed.

The next day, we all went for a swim, leaving a now more placid Mother pottering about the garden with her seed catalogue. The sea was bath temperature and you had to swim out and then dive down some five or six feet to find water cool enough to be refreshing. Afterwards we lay in the shade of the olives, letting the salt water dry to a silken crustiness on our bodies.

'You know,' said Margo, 'I've been thinking.'

Larry looked at her with disbelief.

'What have you been thinking?' he enquired.

'Well, I think you made a mistake with the professor. I don't think he was Mother's type.'

'Well, I was only fooling,' said Larry, languidly. 'I was always against this idea of her remarrying, but she seemed so convinced that she should.'

'You mean it was *Mother's* idea?' asked Leslie, baffled.

'Of course,' said Larry. 'When you get to her age and start planting passion flowers all over the place, it's obvious, isn't it?'

'But think of the consequences if she'd married the professor,' Margo exclaimed.

'What consequences?' Leslie asked, suspiciously.

'Well, she would have gone to live with him in Athens,' said Margo.

'So, what about it?'

'Well, who would cook for us? Lugaretzia?'

'God forbid!' Larry said, with vehemence.

'Do you remember her cuttlefish soup?' asked Leslie.

'Please don't remind me,' said Margo. 'All those accusing eyes floating there, looking up at you – ugh!'

'I suppose we could have gone to Athens and lived with her and Erisipolous, or whatever he's called,' said Leslie.

'I don't think he would have taken kindly to having four children foisted on to him in his declining years,' observed Larry.

'Well, I think we've got to turn Mother's mind to other things,' said Margo, 'not marriage.'

'She seems hell bent on it,' said Larry.

'Well, we must unbend her,' said Margo. 'Try and keep her on the rails, watch out she doesn't meet too many men. Keep an eye on her.'

'She *seems* all right,' Leslie said, doubtfully.

'Planting passion flowers,' Larry pointed out.

'*Exactly*,' said Margo. 'We must watch her. I tell you, where there's no smoke, there's no fire.'

So bearing this in mind we all dispersed and went about our various tasks, Larry to write, Margo to work out what to do with seventeen yards of red velvet she had bought at a knock-down price, Leslie to oil his guns and make cartridges and me to try and catch a mate for one of my toads, for the marital affairs of my animals were infinitely more important to me than those of my mother.

Three days later, hot, sweaty and hungry, after an unsatisfactory hunt for Leopard snakes in the hills, I arrived back at the villa just when Antoine de Vere was decanted by Spiro from the Dodge. He was wearing an enormous sombrero, a black cloak with a scarlet lining and a suit of pale blue corduroy. He stepped out of the car, closed his eyes, raised his arms to the heavens and intoned in a deep, rich voice, 'Ah! The majesty that is Greece,' and inhaled deeply. Then he swept off his sombrero and looked at me, dishevelled and surrounded by dogs, all of whom were growling ominously. He smiled, a flash of teeth in his brown face, so perfect they might have been newly constructed. His hair was curly and glistening. His eyes were large and shiny, the colour of a newly emerged horse chestnut, and under them the skin was dark like a plum. He was undeniably handsome, one had to admit, but in what Leslie would have described as a dago-ish sort of way.

'Ah!' he said, pointing a long finger at me. 'You must be Lawrence's baby brother.'

From not particularly liking him at first sight, I had been willing to give him a chance, but now my opinion dropped to zero. I had become used to being described in a variety of derogatory ways by both my family and our friends, and I had adopted a stoical attitude to these unkind, untrue and probably slanderous assaults on my character. But no one had ever had the temerity to call me 'baby' before. I was wondering which room he was occupying and whether the insertion of a dead water-snake (which I happened to possess) into his bed would be advantageous, when Larry emerged and whisked Antoine away to the kitchen to meet Mother.

The next few days were, to say the least of it, interesting. Within twenty-four hours Antoine had succeeded in alienating the whole family with the exception – to our astonishment – of Mother. Larry was obviously bored with him and made only the most desultory attempt at being polite. Leslie's opinion was that he was a bloody dago and should be shot and Margo thought he was fat, old and greasy. But Mother for some inexplicable reason apparently found him charming. She was constantly asking him to tour the garden with her and suggest where she should plant things, or inviting him to the kitchen to taste the casserole she was making and to suggest what ingredients to add. She even went so far as to have Lugaretzia, moaning like a Roman galley slave, hobble up three flights of stairs carrying an enormous tray loaded down with enough eggs, bacon, toast, marmalade and coffee to feed a regiment. This was a luxury never afforded us unless we were ill and so, not unnaturally, our dislike of Antoine grew. He appeared to be totally oblivious of our ill-concealed feelings and dominated every conversation and made meal-times intolerable. The personal pronoun had obviously been invented for him, and nearly every sentence began with 'I think' or 'I believe', 'I know' or 'I am of the opinion'. We were counting the days to his departure.

'I don't like it,' said Margo, worriedly. 'I don't like the way he hangs around Mother.'

'Or the way she hangs around him,' said Leslie.

'Nonsense. The man's a bloody bore. He's worse than the professor,' Larry said. 'Anyway, he's going soon, thank God.'

Well, you mark my words, there's something fishy going on,' said Margo. 'There's many a trick between cup and glass.' My sister liked proverbs, but invariably gave her own version of them which tended to be confusing.

'I saw them walking on the hillside yesterday,' observed Leslie, 'and he was plucking flowers for her.'

'There you are, you see,' said Margo. 'Giving flowers to women always means something.'

'I gave a lot of flowers to a woman once and she wasn't a bit grateful,' Larry said.

'Why wasn't she? I thought women liked flowers,' asked Leslie.

'Not in the form of a wreath,' explained Larry. 'As she was dead I suppose one cannot be too harsh in judgement. I'm sure if she'd been alive she would have put them in water.'

'I do wish you'd take things seriously,' said Margo.

'I take wreaths very seriously,' Larry said. 'In America they hang them on doors at Christmas. I suppose to remind you how lucky you are not to be underneath them.'

To our astonishment, Spiro arrived before breakfast the following morning and Antoine, wearing his sombrero, cloak and blue suit, was whisked away, presumably into town. The mystery was explained to us by Mother when we sat down to breakfast.

'Where's Antoine gone?' asked Larry, deftly trepanning a boiled egg. 'I suppose it's too much to hope he's gone for good?'

'No, dear,' said Mother placidly, 'he wanted to do some shopping in town and, anyway, he thought it would save embarrassment if he was not here while I talked to you all.'

'Talked to us? Talked to us about what?' asked Margo in alarm. 'You know some time ago you children were suggesting I got married again,' Mother began, busily pouring out tea and orange juice. 'Well, at the time I was very annoyed, because, as you know, I said I would never marry again as no man could measure up to your father.'

We sat as still as four pebbles.

'I gave the matter considerable thought,' she continued, 'and I decided that you, Larry, were right. I think you do need a father to exert discipline and to guide you. Just having me is not enough.'

We sat as though mesmerized. Mother sipped her tea and put down her cup.

'There are not many choices on Corfu as you know, and I was really at my wits' end. I thought of the Belgian Consul, but he speaks only French and if he proposed I wouldn't understand him. I thought of Mr Kralefsky but he's so devoted to his mother and I doubt whether he'd want to get married. I thought of Colonel Velvit, but I think his interests lie in other directions than ladies. Well, I was almost giving up in despair when Antoine arrived.'

'Mother!' exclaimed Margo in horror.

'Now be quiet, dear, and let me go on. Well, from the word go we were attracted to each other. I don't suppose you all noticed.'

'Oh, yes we did,' said Leslie, 'bloody breakfast in bed, fawning all over the bastard.'

'Leslie, dear, I will not have you use that word about your step-father, or one who I hope will become your step-father in due course.'

'I don't believe it,' said Larry. 'I've always said women were half-witted, but not as stupid as that. Marrying Antoine would get you the Nobel Prize for idiocy.'

'Larry, dear, there's no need to be rude. Antoine has many fine qualities. And anyway, I'm the one who's going to marry him, not you.'

'But you can't marry him, he's horrible,' Margo wailed, on the verge of tears.

'Well, not at once,' said Mother. 'He and I have talked it over. We both agree that too many people rush into marriage and then regret a hasty decision.'

'You'd certainly regret this one,' said Larry.

'Yes, well, as I say, we've talked it over and we've decided that what would be best is for us to live together in Athens for a while and get to know each other.'

'Live with him in Athens? You mean *live in sin*?' asked Margo, horrified. 'Mother, you can't. It would be bigamy.'

'Well, it wouldn't be exactly sin,' Mother explained, 'not if we're planning to get married.'

'I must say that's the most novel excuse for sin I've ever heard,' said Larry.

'Mother, you can't do this,' said Leslie. 'The man's *awful*. You might think of us for a change.'

'Yes, Mother, think what people will say,' said Margo. 'It'll be too embarrassing when people ask where you are to say you're living in sin in Athens with that – that – that –'

'Bastard,' supplied Leslie.

'And a boring one,' added Larry.

'Now, look here,' Mother said. 'If you go on like this you'll get me seriously annoyed. All you children could provide by way of a husband for me was a drunken old fool with a name as long as the alphabet. Now I have chosen Antoine and there's no more to be said. He has all the qualities I admire most in a man.'

'You mean like tediousness, sloth, vanity?' asked Larry.

'Greasy hair?' asked Margo.

'A snore like bloody thunder?' asked Leslie.

I did not make my contribution for I felt Mother would not be swayed by my comment that anyone who called me 'baby' deserved to be strangled at birth.

'It will of course mean a changed way of life for all of us,' Mother explained, pouring herself another cup of tea. 'Gerry as the youngest will come to live with me and Antoine so that he can benefit from Antoine's example. Leslie, you and Margo are quite old enough to stand on your own feet, so I suggest you both go back to England and find yourselves congenial jobs.'

'Mother! You can't mean it!' Margo gasped.

'There's no such thing as a congenial job,' said Leslie, aghast.

'And what about me?' Larry asked. 'What future have you and that barbaric fool planned out for me?'

'Oh, that's the *good* thing,' Mother said, triumphantly. 'Antoine's got a friend in Lithuania who owns a newspaper. Apparently it's got a circulation of several hundred. Antoine is sure he can get you a job as a – a – I think it's called a composer. Anyway, it's one of those people who put all those little bits of type together and then it makes a printed page.'

'Me?' Larry exploded. 'You want me to become a bloody *compositor*!'

'Language, dear,' said Mother, automatically. 'I don't see what's wrong with that. As Antoine knew you wanted to be a writer he thought it would be the perfect job for you. After all, everyone has to start at the bottom.'

'I'd like to start at his bottom and kick it straight up through his bloody skull,' said Leslie, infuriated. 'What does he know about congenial jobs?'

'Well, dear, something that appeals to you – something that suits your character,' Mother explained.

'Like assassination,' Larry suggested, 'and then he could practise on Antoine.'

'I can see that none of you are in a mood to be sensible,' Mother said, with dignity. 'So we'll stop discussing it. But my mind is made up and so you had all better get used to the idea. I shall be in the kitchen if you want to talk seriously. I am cooking Antoine a prawn curry for tonight. It's one of his favourite dishes.'

In silence, we all sat and watched her as she made her way, humming to herself, through the tangerine trees and into the house.

'I simply don't believe it,' said Larry. 'She must have gone dotty. I am sure she's gone dotty. Look at all those round-the-bend relatives we've got. It's in the family. We must resign ourselves to a life of strait-jackets and padded cells.'

'She's *not* dotty,' Margo said. 'I know when Mother's being dotty and when she's not. I can tell.'

'Well, you above all people should be able to,' remarked Larry.

'I think it's serious,' Leslie said. 'If she wants to marry the man I suppose we can't stop her, although I think it's a bit selfish. But for her to suggest we go out and get *jobs*, I think that is *really* carrying things too far.'

74

'I agree,' said Larry. 'The disintegration of family life starts when the children begin to behave normally, and their mother abnormally. Still we always have Spiro's remedy to fall back on.'

'You mean cement sandals?' asked Margo, wide-eyed.

'Boots,' corrected Leslie.

'But wouldn't we be accessories?' asked Margo. 'I mean, after all, it is something like murder when you kill someone like that, isn't it? I mean, you couldn't just say that he stepped into the buckets by accident and then fell off the boat, could you? I mean, I don't think anyone would believe you. I mean, I think they might get suspicious. I mean, I don't think it's a very *safe*. idea. And, anyway, I don't think Antoine if you asked him – and of course we couldn't – would really like the idea anyway. I think he wouldn't want to get us into trouble with the police and things. I mean, I think that he's basically nice, but it's just that he's horrible and he wants to marry Mother and spoil everything.'

'Well, that's succinct,' Larry observed.

'We'll have to do *something*,' Leslie said, worriedly, 'or we'll have that damned man interfering with everything.'

'Yes, our private lives will become public,' said Margo. 'We'll be going around looking over our shoulders all the time.'

'You can't look over both shoulders at once,' corrected Leslie, a stickler for realism.

'You can if you're frightened enough,' Margo said. 'At least I can.'

'We'll have another go at her at lunch,' Larry said. 'Try and show her the error of her ways.'

'D'you think a trip to the local lunatic asylum would do the trick?' Margo suggested. 'That would show her the error of her ways.

'How?' Leslie enquired.

'Well, it would show her what she's in danger of becoming if she doesn't give up this ridiculous idea of marriage to Antoine.'

'Wouldn't work. Every time I pass that place all the inhabitants look as happy as sandboys,' Leslie said. 'No, you'd probably have Mother and Antoine moving in with them. I mean, if they *have* to live in sin it's better they do it in Athens which is far away and not in a lunatic asylum on our very doorstep. It would look bad. People would talk.'

'I shall think of something,' Larry said, and stalked off to his room.

'Well, at any rate it will give you something to do with all that damned velvet you bought,' Leslie observed.

'Do what with it?' Margo enquired.

'You can make Mother her wedding dress out of it.'

'Oh, you do make me sick,' exclaimed Margo, and went off in a huff.

At lunch the assault recommenced, but Mother remained placid but firm.

'You realize you're ruining our lives?' asked Larry.

'Well, I didn't complain when I was left a widow with four children to bring up, dear, did I?'

'How could you complain? We enriched *your* life, and anyway if we hadn't enriched it and made you miserable instead, that would have been just one life ruined. What you're proposing now is the ruination of *four* lives,' said Larry.

'Yes,' agreed Leslie, 'I mean, if we did something like that you'd call us jolly selfish.'

'Yes,' added Margo, 'and it's not as if you *need* to get married. After all, you've got us. Most women would be only too pleased to have four children like us.'

'Well if you meet one I would be very glad if you would introduce me to her,' said Mother frigidly. 'I'm going to have my siesta.'

At tea time we fared no better.

'You realize what people will say when they see you've married a younger man?' Larry asked.

'Antoine is exactly my age, dear.'

'But he *looks* much younger. I don't know if you've peeped into the mirror recently, but you are showing distinct signs of decay. People will say you have married a young gigolo.'

'Isn't that something you play?' asked Margo, mystified.

'No, that's a piccolo,' Leslie explained.

'A gigolo is a sort of dago who goes round making suggestions to women of a certain age.

'What sort of suggestions?' asked Margo.

'Filthy suggestions,' Leslie said, comprehensively.

'Has Antoine been making filthy suggestions to Mother? Oh, I think that's loathsome,' exclaimed Margo. 'It's bad enough them living in sin without having filthy suggestions as well. Mother, really, I think it's too much. You're behaving like something out of *Lady Latterly's Brother*.'

'I do wish you children would all be quiet,' said Mother firmly. 'Antoine has behaved like a perfect gentleman, otherwise I would not have contemplated marrying him. But I've decided to and that's final. Now I'm going to attend to the curry.'

She went off to the huge, subterranean kitchen, where Lugaretzia moaned like someone stretched on the rack.

'There's nothing for it, we'll have to have it out with Antoine. We'll just have to tell him we don't accept him in the role of step-anything,' said Larry.

'Yes, we're four to one,' Leslie pointed out.

'Four to two,' said Margo, 'there's Mother.'

'Mother doesn't count,' said Leslie.

'After all, we have a perfect right,' Larry explained. 'We're doing it for *her* good, *her* happiness. We would never forgive ourselves if we didn't save her from her own stupidity.'

'Yes,' said Margo, 'imagine people saying we understand your mother is living in sin with a piccolo.'

'Gigolo,' Leslie corrected.

'We'll just have to wait until he gets back,' said Larry grimly. 'Yes, and we can really get down to the crutch of the matter,' said Margo.

The beauty of our extremely long driveway was that we could hear and see people coming long before they arrived and when they were bores we all simply vanished into the olive groves and left Mother to entertain them. Spiro's car was equipped with an enormous ancient rubber bulb horn, roughly the size of a large melon, which, when squeezed, emitted a honking sound similar to that of an affronted bull deprived of his nuptial rights, a sound so loud and fearsome it could miraculously make even a Corfu donkey move out of the way. As he entered the drive some half a mile away, he always played a sort of symphony on the horn so that we would know he was coming. Thus were we apprised of Antoine's return and assembled belligerently on the front veranda to do battle. Never did a man have a colder, more implacable and more hostile group to face, a group that emanated enmity as vibrant as seventy-nine Bengal tigresses would produce in defence of their young.

'Ah,' said Mother, hurrying out on to the veranda, 'I *thought* I heard Spiro's horn. So Antoine is back – how lovely.'

The car drew to a halt below us and, to our indescribable disgust, Antoine swept off his hat and blew a kiss to Mother.

'Dear lady, I have returned,' he said. 'Brandy, champagne, flowers for you and little Margo and èclairs – chocolate ones – for our little Gerry. I think I have forgot nothing.'

'Except how to speak English,' Larry observed.

Antoine leapt from the car and, in a fine swirl of cloak, raced up the steps and kissed Mother's hand.

'You have told them?' he asked, anxiously.

'Yes,' said Mother.

Antoine turned to us as a lion-tamer might turn to a troupe of maladjusted beasts of the jungle.

'Ah, my dear ones,' he said, throwing wide his arms as if to embrace us all. 'My adorable adopted family. No man on earth has been so lucky as to have four such saint-like children given to him, as well as a mother who is a gift from heaven.'

The saint-like children glowered at him like an open furnace while Mother simpered.

'Oh, what joy it will be for us,' Antoine continued, apparently oblivious of the hostility. 'I shall be able to help in every way as a father. You, dear Larry, I will be able to give you advice on your writing. Leslie, I feel we should lead you away from this obsession with guns and turn your mind to higher things – perhaps a career in banking or something solid like that, eh? And you, dearest

Margo, so gauche, so naive, we will see what we can do about making you presentable. And little Gerry – such a ragamuffin, with all his silly animals. I am sure we can make something of him. Even the most unlikely material can be moulded to resemble a human being. Oh, what *fun* we shall have sharing our new lives together.'

'Oh, Antoine, it will be wonderful!' mother exclaimed.

Antoine turned to her.

'Yes, it will be wonderful, and you, my dear Louella – I mean Lucy – Lucinda – I mean . . . he broke off and stamped his foot. 'Damn, *damn*, *damn*,' he said.

Mother started to laugh.

'*Damn, damn, damn*,' repeated Antoine. 'This was my big scene and I mucked it up.'

'You did very well up to now,' said Mother, 'and we were going to tell them anyway.'

'Tell us what?' asked Margo, wide-eyed.

'That it was all a bloody leg-pull,' said Larry, irritably.

'A leg-pull?' asked Leslie. 'You mean she's not going to marry Antoine?'

'No, dear,' Mother explained. 'I was very annoyed at the way you were all behaving – very annoyed indeed. After all, I may be your mother but you have no right to meddle in my affairs. I happened to mention this to Antoine to see whether he thought I was being – well, rather harsh, but he agreed with me. So, together we thought up this little plan to teach you all a lesson.'

'I have never heard of anything so devious or so immoral, letting us all suffer in this way, imagining Lugaretzia cooking for us,' said Larry indignantly.

'Yes, you might have thought about *us*,' said Leslie accusingly 'We were all terribly worried.'

'Yes, we were,' agreed Margo. 'After all, we didn't want you to marry any old Tom, Dick or Harry.'

'Or Antoine,' said Larry.

'Well, Antoine played his part wonderfully, in fact he acted so well I began to dislike him a bit myself,' Mother said.

'I can have no greater praise,' said Antoine.

'Well, I think it was perfectly horrible of you to keep us all in suspension,' said Margo. 'I think the least you can do is to promise us you won't get married without our consent.'

'But I don't mind not being married,' said Mother, 'and in any case it would be very difficult to find anyone to measure up to your father. And if I *did* find anyone to compare with him, I'm afraid he would never, ever, propose.'

'Why not?' asked Margo, suspiciously.

'Well, dear, what man in his right mind would take on four children like you?' asked Mother.

Ludwig

It has always been said by the British that the Germans have no sense of humour. I have always suspected this of being a sweeping generalization and, like most sweeping generalizations, probably untrue. My very limited experience with the German race had not led me towards the belief that they were overwhelmingly humorous but then, as I have generally been discussing the wisdom teeth of chimpanzees or ingrowing toe-nails in elephants with a German zoo director, it is easy to see why humour has not crept into the conversation. But nevertheless, I felt that somewhere there must lurk a German with a sense of humour, in the same way that one always feels that somewhere there must lurk an English hotel that can produce good food. I felt that the fact that they were classed as humourless must have percolated through to them and added to their many complexes, but also that the younger German, horrified by this slander, might, by now, with his amazing technical skills, have manufactured a sense of humour. So I was quite prepared, should our paths cross, to deal with him (or, preferably, her) with the utmost tenderness and to assure him (or her) that I did not believe this foul calumny. As always happens when you make altruistic vows like this, your chance comes sooner than you think.

I found myself having extreme marital difficulties and, as this sort of home atmosphere is not conducive to the efforts that go into writing a book, I packed my things and went off to the south coast town of Bournemouth, where I had lived as a young man. It was sufficiently remote to make it unlikely that I would be worried by bores as it was out of season. In fact, for most of the time I was there, I was the only resident guest. It gives you a very curious feeling, being the only guest in a large hotel, as if you were the last person left on the *Titanic*. It was here that I met the redoubtable Ludwig and, if he did not restore my sanity – I never had very much of that, anyway – he certainly restored my sense of humour, though he was totally unaware of his good deed.

On my first morning, before going out to sample the delights of the town, I made my way to the bar at an hour when I thought it was lawful for the democratic British to imbibe intoxicating drinks without risk of arrest, only to find to my chagrin that the bar was firmly shut. Muttering uncomplimentary things about the fatuity of the licensing laws, I was turning away when I saw approaching me a youngish man in striped trousers, dark coat and a delicately frilled white shirt whose brilliance would have shamed the Arctic, embossed with a bow tie as neat as any butterfly. Obviously, he came fairly high in the managerial pecking order. He approached me, his head slightly on one side, his blue eyes wide, innocent and expectant. He had, I noticed, started to go prematurely bald and so he had, with great skill, grown his back hair long, combed it forward, and had it cut to a pointed sort of fringe, like a widow's peak, which, with his bony, rather handsome face, had a very good effect. It made him look rather like a young Napoleon.

'Is there anything wrong, sir?' he asked, and from his accent I felt he must be German.

'What time does the bar open?'

If he had told me that I would have to wait until twelve o'clock, I was more than prepared to tell him in detail what I thought of British licensing laws, of the drinking habits of the British as compared with those on the Continent, and to end up by saying that I thought they had passed some masterly bill or other in order to allow grown-up people to drink in their hotels at any hour they liked. However, he took the wind out of my sails.

'The barman has not yet arrived, sir,' he said, apologetically. 'But if you want a drink, I will open the bar for you.'

'Oh,' I said. 'Are you sure it's all right? I mean, I don't want to put you to any trouble.'

'No trouble at all, sir,' he said, suavely, 'if you will wait while I get the key.'

He presently got the key, opened the bar and poured me out the lager I desired.

'Will you join me?' I asked.

'That is very kind of you, sir,' he said, smiling, his blue eyes lighting up with pleasure. 'I will have the same.'

We drank in silence for a while and then I asked him what his name was.

'Ludwig Dietrich,' he said and added, a touch defensively, 'I am a German.'

'Alas,' I said, with regret I did not feel, 'I have only visited Germany once, for a very short time, so I can't say that I know it.'

I did not say that I had found the hotel staff boorish, the food inedible, and the whole experience like being encased in a suet pudding for three days; I might just have been unfortunate. However, I decided that maybe here stood the German I was seeking, the German with a sense of humour. So, after having a couple of beers with Ludwig, like some fisherman baiting a pool, I tried him out with some crumbs of humour. True, they were simple crumbs, but he laughed and my soul expanded like a rose. I, of all mortals, was the lucky one. I had found the crock of gold at the end of the rainbow. I had found the only German with a sense of humour, rare as a man with six heads. Alas, I was to learn that two laughs in a bar, like a couple of mal-orientated swallows, do not make a summer.

When I left him, I sallied forth into Bournemouth to revisit some of the scenes of my youth and gloat over the cultural treasures of this most smug of south coast resorts. To my horror, I discovered that in twenty-five years so many changes had taken place that I hardly recognized anything.

However, certain things remained intact. There were the Pleasure Gardens, for instance, with their well-ordered flowerbeds, their rockeries, waterfalls and ponds – the ponds reflectionless with thin ice, the rockeries padded with cushions of snow from the last fall, speckled with brave canary-yellow and mauve crocuses. There was the pier, windswept with foam-chained waves rolling under its iron legs and dying in snow-like froth scallops on the beach. There was the Pavilion, that throbbing heart of Bournemouth culture, where I had once had to chase a white Pekinese puppy through the indignant legs of music-lovers endeavouring to enjoy Mozart.

I remembered the girl responsible for this, her delicious nose and her delicious use of the English language. Should I phone her up, I wondered? Then I realized that I did not know her whereabouts. I turned, and headed into the town. The wind was icy but the sky was blue and the sunlight daffodil yellow with some heart in it. I made my way through the arcade, still intact I was glad to see, and opposite, to my great delight, my favourite pub, the Victoria Bar. I entered its warm interior; with its long bar well polished, its red velvet sofas and chairs, its strange, wrought-iron tables painted gold, it was as I remembered it. I ordered a pint of draught Guinness, dark as an Abyssinian maiden, and with a white head on it like a burst of May blossom, and sat watching the sun flood through the great glory of the pub, the windows carefully etched and engraved, three of them. True, they had not Whistler's craftsmanship, but they were gloriously Victorian and work that you could not get repeated now. The bar was full of Dickensian characters such as only congregate in English pubs of this sort. Old ladies with faces like walnuts, crouched comfortably over their port and lemon; a tall, lean-faced man with a coal black coat and a velvet collar and wide-brimmed black hat (some faded thespian from the twenties) eyeing, like a pale shrike, any good-looking young man who came in; two men deep in conversation, their hands protectively curled round their pints, while at their feet, snuffling panting and exuberant, an Old English bulldog sat, exuding bonhomie to everyone who passed by doing a hula with its backside that would have been envied in Bali; a little old lady who must have been nearly ninety, wearing a hat in shocking pink shaped like a policeman's helmet, with matching gloves and bootees and silver stockings, talking earnestly to a very stout lady wearing a black hat with ostrich plumes in it, and a fur coat that looked as if it had been ripped untimely from a very ancient musk ox. The air was redolent of ale and port and various spirit smells, as a good French hotel is redolent of well-cooked meals. Like a beautiful woman enhanced by perfume, the bar wafted to you the delicate scents of a million drinks enjoyed. At any moment, as I supped the creamy darkness of my Guinness, I expected Sherlock Holmes, trailed by a bewildered, puzzled Watson, to appear and voice the crisp comment: When you want to know anything, my dear Watson, go to the local pub.

Reluctantly, I finished my drink and went outside into the cold. I paused for a moment, uncertain where to go. The only improvement I could see to Bournemouth was that now it had become almost a university town and so whilst, in my day, all you saw in the streets were portly brigadiers and elderly ladies, now you were greeted and warmed by the sight of woollyheaded, chocolate-brown Africans, dark, sloe-eyed Iranians and clusters of beautiful Chinese and Japanese girls, like flocks of butterflies or enchanting pale amber birds, their hands, finely boned as fans, doing ballets of explanation as they trotted along.

I decided I was cold and lonely, so I would go back to the hotel and write until it was time for lunch. I sat in the cocktail bar, all glitter and chrome, and had another Guinness. I wrote assiduously for a while, then I read the paragraph I had written. It leered evilly at me in the way first paragraphs do, when all the words have got together and are telling you that no matter *what* you do they are going to make sure you don't like them; nor are you going to be any more successful with the next paragraph. Mentally I ran through my fairly extensive repertoire of bad language in English, Greek, Spanish and French – my only claim to being quadrilingual. Then I ordered a double brandy. It was a mistake. Lager, Guinness and brandy are uplifting things on their own but consumed, as it were, in an omelette, they have a depressant effect. The handsome Italian barman, Luigi (whom I was to get to know better later on), took one look at my gloomy face and moved tactfully down to the other end of the bar and polished glasses assiduously. He had known the brandy was a mistake. I was just wondering which form of suicide was the least painful when Ludwig materialized at my elbow.

'Did you have a pleasant morning, sir?' he asked, looking at me anxiously.

I laid down my pen and drained my brandy.

'If,' I said carefully, 'you mean did I enjoy revisiting the scenes of my youth and being made to feel approximately eighty years old, the answer is no.'

'You are not eighty years old?' he queried in astonishment. 'You look much younger'

'Thank you,' I said. 'As a matter of fact, if I avoid mirrors, I can pretend I am a handsome and well-preserved forty, whereas honesty compels me to admit that I am in a much older and more decrepit condition.'

'Well,' said Ludwig, determined to repair any damage he might have done to my morale, 'you do not look it'

'Thank you,' I said. 'Have a drink.'

'Thank you,' he said. 'I will have a gin.'

I ordered a gin and, in a spirit of bonhomie, another brandy. We toasted each other.

'Gin,' I observed, 'is very bad for you. Why do you risk certain death by drinking it?'

A worried look spread over Ludwig's face.

'Gin? Is bad?' he asked anxiously. 'Why?'

'Don't you read the *Lancet*?' I asked in simulated astonishment.

'What is lancet?' he asked.

'The greatest medical journal in the world,' I said. 'Tells you everything . . . every new discovery. . . . gives instructions to doctors. You know, how to pour boiling pitch over an amputated leg stump . . that sort of thing. All the doctors read it.'

'So,' said Ludwig, 'it is a sort of doctors' magazine?'

'You could call it that,' I said, wondering what the BMA would think of this description. 'But of course, it only has pictures of arteries and glands and leprosy and so forth. No nudes or pornographic stuff, really, except that some of the text goes pretty close to the knuckle, if you'll pardon the anatomical allusion.'

'What does the magazine say about gin?' asked Ludwig, regarding his glass with suspicion.

'Well,' I said, 'it tends to make you bald, for one thing.'

His hand fluttered nervously up to stroke his carefully cultivated widow's peak.

'And then it gives you bad breath, it rots your teeth, and you get severe attacks of housemaid's knee,' I concluded.

'What is housemaid's knee?' he asked.

'Well, housemaids would get that,' I said. 'You would probably get under-manager's knee, which is the same but more painful.'

'When did you discover this?' asked Ludwig.

'Quite recently. Have another drink.'

'Thank you. I will have a lager,' he said. 'Lager is good, no?'

I sighed. My German had not a sense of humour or, if he had, it was lying dormant. Perhaps I could, by careful dowsing, uncover the bubbling springs of merriment.

'Don't take any notice of me,' I said. 'I like to joke a lot.'

'Joke,' said Ludwig seriously, as if it was a word that he was unfamiliar with. 'Ah, yes, it is good to joke; one cannot be serious all the time. Joking makes one laugh.'

I sipped my brandy and contemplated my new acquaintance. He was not unattractive looking, with wide, soft, earnest blue eyes but with the faint air of a nervous rabbit. He gave me the impression that, without actually doing so, he was constantly looking over his shoulder for an imaginary enemy, or, perhaps, a germ.

'May I call you Ludwig?' I asked. 'I am called Gerry.'

'With pleasure,' he said, and smiled at me beguilingly and gave a tiny bow. I decided to test him out.

'Tell me, Ludwig,' I asked, 'who, in this hotel, do I complain to?' A look of consternation spread over his face.

'Complain?' he asked. 'You want to complain?'

His fingers twitched round his glass as though his worst fears had been realized.

'I mean,' I explained, 'if I want to complain, who do I complain to?'

'You tell me your complaint,' he said eagerly. 'I will do what you want.'

'Look,' I said patiently, 'suppose I don't like the colour of the carpet in my room, who would I complain to?'

'I can change the furniture,' he said, eagerly, pacifyingly. 'But the carpet is fixed to the floor. But I could move you to a room with a different coloured carpet tomorrow.'

'I don't want to change. I like the colour of my carpet.'

'But you said . . .' he began.

'I was joking about the carpet,' I explained.

He had the look of someone who has just escaped from under the wheels of a fast-moving vehicle.

'Joking,' he said. 'Ah, yes, joking.' He laughed with nervous relief.

'However,' I said, 'there is the shower.'

His relief evaporated and his nervousness returned. 'The shower? What is wrong with the shower?' he asked anxiously.

'I am not insured against being blinded by a jet of scalding hot water every time I turn it on,' I explained. 'Also, it only points in one direction, and it is tedious to have to stand out in the hallway to get the full benefit of it.'

'This is another joke?' he enquired hopefully.

'Alas, no,' I said, mournfully. 'This morning I was hit between the eyes with a jet of hot water of such ferocity and heat that I almost telephoned reception for a guide dog to get me down to breakfast.'

'I will have it fixed immediately,' he said and, gulping down his drink, he sped away like a tumbleweed of exposed nerve endings.

I did not see him again until late that evening. Unwisely, perhaps, I was celebrating the eve of my birthday with brandy, a liquid which can make your brain crystal clear, as though illuminated by some strange fire, but it can also make your tongue loquacious and unwise. I was sitting in the gigantic lounge, silent and deserted, endeavouring to write, when he suddenly materialized in an unnerving way in front of me, the thick, soft carpets having muffled his footsteps like snow.

'Hello,' he said, gazing at me earnestly. 'You are sitting up late.'

'I can't sleep and so I am writing,' I said. 'Press the bell and a strange night porter will appear like a genie out of a bottle, bearing brandy for me and whatever you want.'

He pressed the bell and sat down opposite me, regarding me with a slightly worried expression.

'You write a lot,' he observed.

As I had been scowling at the one sentence I had written in the last half hour, while trying to think what to follow it with, I greeted this observation with exasperation. I slammed my notebook shut.

'Yes,' I said, 'I write a lot. Unfortunately, the number of foreigners in Bournemouth is affecting my style.'

'Style? What is?' he enquired.

'My writing.'

'It is affected by foreigners?' he asked, puzzled.

'Naturally,' I said. 'Any proper Englishman is affected by foreigners, don't you know that? Why the Almighty didn't make everyone an Englishman defeats me.'

'But how foreigners affect you?' he asked enquiringly.

'Just because they're not English,' I said. 'Look here, I go out into the streets, and what do I see? English men and women? No, a lot of Japs and Chinese, Iranians, Abyssinians and Basutolanders. Then I come back to the hotel and what do I discover? Englishmen? No. A filthy Italian barman named Luigi, who looks as though his great-great-grandfather was Machiavelli. A cohort of waiters who are all filthy Spaniards or filthy Italians or filthy Portuguese – and I have no doubt that there is a filthy French frog lurking somewhere, reeking of garlic!'

'But I am a foreigner,' said Ludwig.

'Just what I mean,' I said. 'You're a filthy Hun. It's carrying this Common Market thing too far. Soon Britain will be so full of filthy foreigners that I'll be forced to go abroad to enjoy the English.'

He gazed at me for a long moment, and then laughed.

'Filthy Hun,' he repeated, smiling broadly. 'Now I know you joke.'

I sighed.

'Yes,' I admitted. 'I am joking.'

'What kind of books do you write?' he asked.

'Sexy novels,' I explained. 'Novels about sex maniacs raping and plundering their way through hotels like this.'

There was a moment's pause and then he smiled.

'You are again joking, I can tell,' he said, with satisfaction.

The night porter appeared, and before Ludwig could say anything, I ordered two large brandies. He looked shocked and was about to protest, when I held up my hand.

'Celebration,' I said, glancing at the clock.

'Celebration?' he asked. 'What for?'

'In one minute, it will be midnight,' I said, 'and then it will be my birthday. Jollity, gaiety, and all that sort of stuff. I should stand well back if I were you; in all probability, I shall turn into a pumpkin or a werewolf, or something.'

'Your birthday?' said Ludwig. 'Really? You are not joking?'

'No, in one minute's time I will have fifty-one glorious misspent years lying behind me.'

The porter brought the drinks. Ludwig and I raised our glasses, and as the hands of the clock reached the twelve, Ludwig rose to his feet and toasted me.

'Congratulations and many other times,' he said.

'Thank you,' I said, 'and the same to you.'

We drank.

'You look worried,' he said, looking worried for me.

'Well, wouldn't you be?' I enquired.

'But why?' he asked.

'Well, here I am, fifty-two and so far nothing has happened to me.'

'But you have only just become fifty-two,' said Ludwig earnestly. 'You can't expect things to happen at once.'

'Why not?' I asked. 'Why shouldn't a dark and voluptuous lady in a see-through nightie suddenly rush into the lounge and ask me to save her from a mad bull?'

'In the hotel?' asked Ludwig. 'How would a bull get in?'

'By the lift,' I said. 'Or maybe it could sneak in, disguised as a chambermaid, and lurk in the lady's bedroom ready to attack her.'

'You are joking again,' said Ludwig, with immense satisfaction, as though he had caught me out cheating at cards. I sighed.

'Tell me, Ludwig,' I asked, 'what made you leave all the bubble and gaiety in Germany to come to Bournemouth? Is the money better?'

'No, no,' he said, 'but in Germany all they do is work, all day, and in the evening they are too tired to do anything. They have no fun.'

'No joking?' I asked, amazed.

'No,' said Ludwig, 'they are too tired.'

'So you escaped to England?'

'Yes, I like England very much,' said Ludwig.

We sat in silence for a bit while I thought moodily of the piece I was writing, which refused to come right.

'You are looking worried again,' said Ludwig, anxiously.

'No. Only my bloody writing won't come right,' I explained. 'That's all. It's called author's constipation. It will pass.'

He looked at me in a slightly embarrassed fashion.

'Tomorrow is my day off,' he said. 'I have a Mercedes car.'

I pondered this apparently disconnected statement and wondered which of us had drunk the most brandy.

'So?' I asked, cautiously.

'I thought that perhaps, since it was your birthday and you are alone in the hotel, you might like a drive,' he explained, blushing slightly.

I sat up.

'What a splendid idea! Do you really mean it?' I asked, touched by his kindness.

'Of course,' he said, his eyes shining at my obvious enthusiasm.

'I tell you what,' I said. 'You come and have lunch with me and then we'll zoom off. Have you ever seen Corfe Castle or the Purbecks?'

'No,' said Ludwig. 'Since my girlfriend, Penny, left, I don't go out much.'

'Good,' I said, 'it's a date. You come and pick me up at twelve and we'll go and have a drink and a good meal and then go and beat up the Purbecks.'

So, punctually at twelve, we met in the hall. Ludwig looked somehow undressed in an open-necked shirt without his bow tie, and a gay sports jacket instead of his formal black coat, but this flamboyant disguise made him no whit the less earnest. We walked down through the Pleasure Gardens to the hotel which, in my opinion, served the nearest approach to good French food in Bournemouth, the Royal Bath Buttery. En route, we went into a pub where the barman, an Irishman, with a bland face but whose dark eyes held the faintest glow in their depths, like a firefly in a velvety black night, had led me to believe that he had found the world a humorous place.

Ludwig took a long time to choose a drink. He wouldn't have gin, for as he explained to the barman, it gave one housemaid's knee. The barman's eyes flicked over me briefly, and I winked. The glow in his eyes deepened and he became appreciative.

Sherry, he said in a deep Irish brogue, gave one gout, so did port.

Beer, I said earnestly, made one fat and, therefore, affected the heart, as did brandy if taken at midday. The barman said that some of his customers who insisted on drinking whisky had their arteries harden up so quickly that they had become quite immobile and stiff all of a sudden, like statues. I said that I'd known this happen with rum, only they became a sort of sticky heap, like molasses. Not to be outdone, the barman said that vodka ate through the intestines and stomach wall; only the other day he'd had a customer pass away because his whole stomach had fallen out on the floor. A terrible mess he'd had to clean up, he sighed, and the poor fellow had been eating bacon and eggs for breakfast. I gave the barman full marks. It is the little artistic touches like this that make a good Irish lie. Ludwig had listened to this exchange with care. Now he examined my face carefully.

'You are both joking?' he asked, so pathetically that I had to admit that we were, so we ordered lagers and the barman joined us.

Soon, Ludwig was telling me how much he was looking forward to his holiday.

'Where are you going?' I asked.

'I would like to go to the south of France,' he said, 'but I can't.'

'Why not?' I asked. 'You've got a fast car and the roads are good. You can get down to Cannes in one day.'

'But I must see my family.'

'Do you want to see them?' I enquired, thinking of the casual way in which our family popped in and out of each other's lives with infrequency and less warning than a cuckoo's sorties on its avian friends.

'No, but it's my family,' he said simply. 'That is why I cannot go to the south of France, where my girlfriend, Penny, is.'

This struck me as carrying filial devotion too far.

'Why not see them on the way back?' I suggested. 'Go and see Penny first.'

Ludwig looked shocked.

'Or,' I continued, 'why not one year say "damn the family", and go to . . . go to . . . Mexico?'

He considered this, while the barman and I waited to see if he would be corrupted.

'I would like to see Mexico,' he said at length. 'But maybe it is too hot. I found Spain very hot.'

'Why didn't you complain to the government?' I asked. He considered this.

'It is not a justifiable complaint,' he explained.

Both the barman and I hoped fervently that this was a joke. It wasn't; it was a plain statement of fact. The barman and I exchanged anguished looks.

'Well,' I said judiciously, 'there are cooler places. Baffinland, for example.'

'Yes?' asked Ludwig with interest.

'Our friend here,' I said, gesturing at the barman, 'now, he can tell you about Baffinland.'

The barman, with a face as expressionless as a pool of tar, picked up a glass and started to polish it.

'Baffinland is cool,' he said softly and earnestly. 'It is so cool they have to make special spirits to drink there, otherwise the bottles burst.'

Ludwig thought about this one for a moment.

'What proof?' he asked.

The barman sighed. I could tell he was now beginning to understand my problem.

'If you went to Baffinland, you would have the hospitality of the Eskimos,' I said, helpfully. 'Vast quantities of blubber, rubbing noses with gay Eskimo wives . . . ?'

'Blubber is what?' asked Ludwig.

'The small, but important, semi-convoluted lower section of the bowel of a whale over the age of consent,' I said.

'When caught during the month of August at full moon when the icebergs start to melt,' said the barman, placidly, and with total conviction, earning my undying admiration.

'By hand harpoon,' I added, greatly daring.

'I don't think I would like that,' said Ludwig. 'It tastes like fish, no? Kippers always make me sick when I am eating them, and I suffer a great thirst.'

I looked at the barman, who gazed back at me with sympathy. 'I've got a right one here,' I said, 'a veritable Hun.'

'You have that, sir,' said the barman. 'I'm thinking a week or two in Dublin would be a fine cure; as good as a mental home, some say.'

'I'll think about it,' I promised.

'Dublin is very wet, isn't it?' asked Ludwig, earnestly enquiring after knowledge.

'Yes,' said the barman. 'The Venice of the north, they call it. That's where they invented the gondola.'

'But I thought . . .' began Ludwig, puzzled.

'Come,' I said, seizing his arm in a firm grip. 'Let's go and have a kipper.'

During an excellent meal, Ludwig unburdened himself to me

about Penny. She was young, she was gay (I strongly suspected she had a sense of humour), but always they were fighting, always.

She was not ready when she should be, always she did not want to do what he suggested and, sin of sins, she left stockings and brassieres lying about on the floor in her efforts to get dressed quickly. He felt that this last habit, combined with a certain age gap, made the idea of marriage impossible, or, if not impossible, suspect. I said I thought that that was exactly what he wanted: someone young, vital, who would argue with him and keep him permanently waist-deep in discarded brassieres and stockings. I said that marriages had been ruined by the wife being too tidy and many others had been saved by a brassiere being dropped at the right moment. He was much struck by the novelty of this idea and, after two bottles of excellent wine, I almost had him and Penny owning their own hotel in Bournemouth, providing she promised not to drop brassieres in the corridors.

'I have written to ask her if she will come up and join me for my holiday,' he confessed.

'And what did she say?'

'She has not replied. It is very worrying,' he said, worrying.

'Stop worrying,' I said firmly. 'If you knew the French postal system like I do, you wouldn't worry at all. The letter saying yes, she loves you will come on your hundredth birthday.'

He looked alarmed.

'Joke,' I explained.

'Ah!' he said, relieved. 'So you think she will agree?'

'Can't fail to,' I assured him. 'Who could resist the advances of a filthy Hun?'

Ludwig, since he knew this joke, laughed uproariously. Then he fell serious.

'You travel a lot?' he asked.

'A fair bit.'

'Does it . . . you know . . . upset you?'

'No. Why?'

'Whenever I am going on holiday, I get very nervous and my bowels suffer,' he confessed. 'The closer it gets to my holiday, the worse it gets. And then, when I go on holiday, it gets so bad that I do not enjoy myself.'

'What you need is a tranquillizer,' I said. 'I'll give you some.'

'They would work?" he asked, hopefully.

'Of course,' I said. 'Remind me – I've got some somewhere. I take them myself sometimes when I've been overdoing it.'

'I'd be very grateful,' he said. 'I want to enjoy my holiday'.

'You will,' I promised, 'and Penny too.'

In good spirits, we set off to the old Sandbanks chain ferry, which is really rather like a curious gateway into another world. As Charon ferries you across the Styx, for far more pleasant reasons the ferry lumbered across the mouth of Poole harbour, island-dotted, sea-bird-flecked, from the glittering beehive hotels of Bournemouth into a piece of pastoral England which did not look as though it had changed since the 1700s. Here, the rolling hillsides were great green meadows, hedged with blackthorns, dark and spiky, tangled as a witch's hair. The ploughed fields, neat and smooth as corduroy, had flocks of rooks and seagulls following the ploughs, as though the farmers were setting the trail for some strange avian paper-chase. The new catkins were lemon yellow, illuminating the hedgerows, and the willows had sealskin buds in profusion. In the tall, stark and leafless trees that rose along the crests of the hills, bare black branches intertwined against the sky to form a blue stained-glass window of great complexity, marred here and there by the early foundations of a rook's or magpie's nest. Ludwig put on his tape-recorder and loud, exuberant, brassy Bavarian music throbbed through the car. One could almost hear the slap of horny hands upon leather breeches and the clump of huge climbing boots as the Bavarians, with gigantic glasses of beer, enjoyed themselves. It made such a contrast to the landscape that we were passing through, that it became amusing.

Then we rounded a corner and before us, on an almost conical mound, set in the declivity between two great green breasts of hills, stood the remains of Corfe Castle, like some huge, rotting dinosaur's tooth embedded in the green gum of the hill upon which it stood. The central block, the only tall piece to have resisted the mines and gunpowder of Cromwell's vandalistic Parliamentarians, now stood up against the blue sky like an admonishing, leprous finger, jackdaw-haunted, somehow macabre and sad at the same time.

We parked the car and walked towards the castle. The cold crisp air and the wine that we had drunk made me feel slightly light-headed. At the entrance two squat fat towers, like pitted beer mugs, guarded a massive arch and to one side, in the remains of the wall, another similar tower leaned out at an acute angle, like a tree that, water-worn or wind-tossed, had been bent over but refused to relinquish its hold on the earth. The charge of powder used to try to destroy it had not been large enough to cope with this bulky chess-piece of Purbeck masonry.

Ahead of us, walking in the same direction, was a tall girl with dark hair. She had those deliciously long legs that only American girls appear to have, racehorse legs, that seem to start at the chin and go on for ever.

I started my lecture on English history for Ludwig's benefit.

'It was here,' I said, pointing to the arch, 'that the first of many murders was done. The dastardly deed was committed by Elfrieda on Ethelred the Unready. He was hunting in the district and he came here to visit his brother. Elfrieda was, of course, his step-mother and was jealous because Ethelred had no Oedipus complex about her. Anyway, as Ethelred the Unready – sometimes called Ethelred the Unsteady when he had been at the mead . . .'

'Mead? What is?' asked Ludwig, who had been following me with close attention.

'Three parts vodka, one part honey-and-water, and a touch of angostura bitters,' I said crisply, and was delighted to see the girl ahead slow down from a long-legged, eager stride to a stroll, the better to hear my lecture.

'Well, Ethelred the Unready galloped over the bridge, under this arch, and greeted his step-mother as warmly as anyone can do without an Oedipus complex. He said he wanted to see his brother. His step-mother said that his brother was down in the dungeons playing thumb-screws and would be called instantly. In the meantime, perhaps Ethelred would have a slug of mead to keep his end up. Ethelred said he would.'

We had now reached the pay box and I could see the girl's face. She was undeniably lovely. She bought a guide-book and she had an American accent. As she turned away, our eyes met. She grinned suddenly, and wagged the guide-book at me.

'Some people,' I said, 'would hardly credit what happened next.'

The girl hesitated and then started slowly up the slope to the main castle mins, but slowly enough that she could still overhear our conversation.

'What happened?' asked Ludwig.

'Well, Elfrieda mixed the mead in a ram's horn cocktail-shaker and handed a horn of it to Ethelred. As he leant down to seize and quaff it, she stuck a knife in his back, an inhospitable action for which he was quite unready, hence his name. She then stuffed his body down a well, hence the origin of the old English saying, "All's well that ends well".'

'The police never caught her?' asked Ludwig.

'No,' I said. 'They spent months finger-printing everybody in the castle with no results. Old Scotland Yard, as it was known then, was completely baffled.'

'And who,' asked Ludwig, determined to get the historical facts straight, 'was this Oedipus complex?'

'An extremely wicked knight, Sir Oedipus, who wanted to marry Elfrieda and gain the throne. He wanted to become Rex, you know. You've heard of the saying "black as the night"?'

'Yes,' said Ludwig.

'They invented the phrase to describe Sir Oedipus,' I said.

The girl, I noticed, had paused within earshot and was studying her guide-book assiduously. I was glad to see that she was holding it upside-down. The man in the ticket office gazed at us reflectively.

'You would not be wanting a guide-book, sir,' he stated, rather than asked, in a lovely Dorset accent you could cut with a knife, like a piece of delicious cheese.

'No, thank you,' I said airily. 'I am familiar with the history of this noble pile.'

So I hear, sir,' he said, twinkling at me. 'Your friend's a foreign gentleman, I take it?'

'German,' I said. 'You know what *they're* like.'

'Oh, aahh,' said the man. 'Oh, aahh. I know all right.'

'You come from Dorset?' asked Ludwig, interestedly.

This was too much for the man's gravity and with a muffled 'Yes sir', he fled to the back of the kiosk.

'Come,' I said to Ludwig. 'We have much to see and the history is fascinating.'

We passed the girl and slowly she started to follow us.

'Now,' I said, as we climbed the grassy slopes towards the castle, 'we will skip a century or two until we come to the point where Henry VIII won the castle from Henry VII in a game of dice.'

On the rich green grass, a small flock of sheep grazed, the ram with great, tightly curled horns like huge ammonites on each side of his skull.

'Now, you know that Henry VIII had only three passions in life,' I continued. 'Women, food and music. Here you see before you the remains of the very flock of sheep that used to be served up to Henry with peas, chipped potatoes and mint sauce. Normally it was chops, but on the days when he had executed a wife or two he'd celebrate with a leg served with rosemary and thyme.'

'They are very dirty,' said Ludwig, gazing at the sheep.

'They keep them dirty so that no one will poach them,' I explained. 'They are washed once a year, on St Omo's Day, in a great ceremony in the castle's sheep-dip.'

'Oh,' said Ludwig.

He gazed around at the huge blocks of fallen masonry and half-demolished walls.

'Where are the kitchens?' he asked.

I led him into a room which I suppose in the old days was where the sentries sat and guarded the second entrance with the draw-bridge into the castle, polishing their bows and arrows and keeping the boiling pitch at the right temperature. The room, which had no roof, was some twenty feet by nine. One end was curved, and in it was set a long narrow arrow-slit like a cross in the thick masonry.

'This,' I said, 'was the great kitchen.'

The American girl had paused just outside.

'But it is small,' said Ludwig.

'Not if you are a skilful cook, and if you have got all the modern conveniences. Henry was very keen on his food, as I told you, and it was more than the cook's life was worth to serve a bad meal, but a good cook can easily produce a banquet in a space like this, seven or ten courses, perhaps. The art of good cookery is tidiness,' I said unctuously, remembering vividly that my wife had said that I was the untidiest cook she had ever met.

'But how did they get the food upstairs?' asked Ludwig, greatly puzzled.

'Through the serving hatch,' I said, pointing at the arrow-slit. 'Tall things, like celery and so on, through the upright, and the trays of the small, flatter stuff, through the cross slit.'

Ludwig stepped forward to examine it.

'It is very extraordinary,' he said.

The American girl looked at me, shook her head reprovingly, grinned and then, to my annoyance, disappeared. I showed Ludwig round the rest of the castle, pouring misinformation into his eager ears and hoping that we might catch up with her, but she had vanished.

Ludwig grew more and more worried. The guest rooms, some eight feet by six, would, he pointed out to me, only hold a moderate-sized double bed without any space to get in and out of the room. How did Queen Elizabeth who, I had informed him, came up for weekends with her father, manage? I said you simply opened the door and jumped into bed. It saved a lot of mucking about, and as the bed took up the whole room, you didn't have to worry about sweeping under it. He was worried, too, by the sanitary arrangements – the remains of a round tower some five hundred yards away from the main castle, perched on the edge of the hill, which I told him served as a ladies' and gents' toilet.

'Why so far away?' he asked.

'Two reasons,' I explained. 'Firstly, as you can see by its position, every time they flushed it, the contents rushed down the hillside into the enemy's camp, causing acute consternation. And, secondly, Henry had it built there as a punishment. He found his courtiers were simply using the battlements and the sentries below were complaining, so Henry had it built out there and everyone, on pain of death, had to use it. I can tell you, on a cold winter's night, it was very effective.'

The American girl had vanished just as completely and as suddenly as a rabbit down a hole, and I felt sad. I thought that, maybe, a few more of my historical gems and we might have made contact. Slowly, we retraced our steps to the entrance, and as we walked down the slope, I glanced up at one part of the castle that remained more or less intact and saw, high above, in the carunculated remains of a window, with the jackdaws drifting round it like ash flakes, the beautiful girl leaning out and watching us. I waved and she waved back. I needed no further encouragement. Making my hands into a trumpet, I shouted;

'Lady fair, it's my day for rescuing beautiful princesses, and I know that you are in distress.'

She considered me gravely, leaned forward, her mane of black hair falling over her shoulders.

'Sir knight, I am in dire distress,' she called melodiously, with that soft American accent. 'How did you know my plight?'

My heart warmed to her.

'Lady, this whole kingdom knows it,' I said, making, as they used to say, a leg. 'I and my jester here have travelled many a weary mile to rescue you from a fate worse than death.'

'What is jester?' asked Ludwig.

'A sort of fool,' I said.

'You mean, an idiot?' he asked, indignantly.

'Sir knight,' called my princess, looking nervously behind her. 'Speak low, I fear the guards may hear.'

'Lady, the fact that your wicked uncle has imprisoned you, so that he may take both your kingdom and your virtue, has come to my ears,' I shouted.

'An idiot is a jester?' asked Ludwig.

'A licensed buffoon,' I said.

'My virtue too?' enquired my princess.

'What is a buffoon?' asked Ludwig.

'Yes, that precious gem that women hold so dear,' I said. 'Your uncle, even now, with black and ferocious brow . . .'

'Is buffoon the same as jester?' asked Ludwig. 'So it means it is three words for idiot.'

'Yes,' I said tersely, for my princess was hanging upon my every word.

'Tell me, fair knight, what is my uncle doing?' she questioned, melodiously.

'He is sitting, at this very moment, planning your doom, madam,' I said. 'But never fear, I will . . .'

'Doom is another word for death?' asked Ludwig.

'Yes,' I said.

'Tell me, fair knight, can I, with your help, avert it?' asked my princess.

'Lady, fear not,' I said. 'No uncle, however incestuous, however depraved, however twisted of soul, backed by a thousand minions, however squat, however hairy, however medieval, whatever the forces ranged against us – we will, with our trusty sword Excalibur . . .'

'You know this girl?' asked Ludwig, with interest.

'Sir Lancelot, 'tis you!' cried the lady in tremulous tones.

''Tis I, madam, and at your service,' I replied.

'You meet her maybe somewhere before?' asked Ludwig.

'Look,' I said, exasperated, 'shut up a minute.'

The jackdaws wheeled about the tower, calling querulously.

'Lady,' I called, 'we have waiting below my trusty steed, my horse Mercedes, upon whose back we will transport you to safety.'

'Mercedes is not *one* horse,' said Ludwig, 'it is twenty in this model.'

'Sir Lancelot, your kindness is equal to your courage,' said my princess.

'Then I shall scale your battlements, kill your guards, and transport you to the village of Ye Bournemouth for a dinner of venison and mead.'

'In Germany, we have much venison,' said Ludwig, 'with dumplings.'

'Alas, Sir Lancelot,' said the princess, 'I fear it cannot be, even though I yearn for mead with vodka and a dash of angostura bitters. In yonder hamlet my betrothed awaits my release and he is of jealous mien.'

'What means "mien"?' asked Ludwig.

'Disposition,' I said. 'Damn! She would be engaged.'

'Mien is plural for men?' asked Ludwig.

'Princess,' I said, sorrowfully, 'you should not have been so precipitate. Remember the adage, "Marry in haste, repent at leisure," and quite apart from that, I had such a hell of a job pulling my sword out of that stone, specially for you.'

She laughed.

'You will find other princesses, I'm sure,' she said. 'Farewell, Sir Lancelot.'

'Farewell, sweet Guinevere,' I said.

'You said you didn't know her,' said Ludwig, as I led him down to the castle gates. 'But how do you know her name?'

'She's Guinevere Smith from Jollytown, Ohio,' I said, 'and I met her in New York. Now let's get back to Bournemouth. The bars will be open.'

'This castle,' said Ludwig, as we made our way towards the arched entrance, 'is not in a very good state of repair.'

'We English like them like this,' I said. 'We like to feel they are a bit on the old side, you know.'

'But on the Rhine,' said Ludwig, 'we have many castles, many beautiful, big castles, and they are all in a very good state of repair.'

Luckily, just by the entrance was standing a rather forlorn wheel-barrow full of gravel.

'There,' I said, pointing at it, 'we are doing something about it. Come back in a year or two and it will look like a Hilton.'

The green of the fields in the fading light had turned to dark emerald, and the ploughed fields had turned a curious deep purple brown. The light on Poole harbour was pink and the gulls, wheeling home to roost, were reflected in the almost smooth waters like snowflakes. Ludwig played some more Bavarian music and thumped the steering wheel as he was not wearing leather knickerbockers.

'Well, it has been a most interesting day,' he said, as we turned into the road leading to the hotel. 'When my parents come over, I will take them to Corfe Castle and tell them everything.'

I felt a little guilty.

'You should buy a guidebook,' I said. 'You'll never remember it all.'

'Yes,' said Ludwig. 'I will do that.'

'And thank you for a lovely day,' I said.

'Thank *you*,' he said, formally.

We garaged the car and, as we were walking towards the hotel, he glanced at me shyly.

'You will not forget those pills, will you?' he asked.

'Of course not,' I said. 'I've packed them somewhere, and I can't find them. But I'll have a proper took tomorrow.'

'Tomorrow is last day,' he reminded me. 'The next day I go on holiday.'

'You shall have them, I promise.'

It was, as it turned out, just as well that I eventually found the tranquillizers. Returning from the cinema, I was surprised to see a dense crowd of people on the pavement and in the road outside the Royal Highcliffe Palace. When I got closer, I could discern in their midst a police car with a pulsating blue light on top, an ambulance and two fire-engines. Ladders from the fire-engines craned up into the sky like the necks of strange prehistoric beasts, and the pavement was covered with hosepipes, like a monstrous brood of newly-hatched pythons. High up on the side of the hotel was the cause of all the commotion, the great neon sign which had, in some mysterious way, caught fire. Although the alarm had been given promptly, by the time the fire was under control all that was left of the sign was YAL HIGH LACE which looked like a chapter heading for one of the Dead Sea Scrolls, or the name of some ancient Chinese philosopher. I pushed my way through the throng and found a distraught Ludwig escorting out a host of large firemen and even larger policemen. He looked so pale, exhausted and guilty, that one would have thought that he had set fire to the sign himself.

'Hello,' I said, cheerfully. 'You've been having a jolly time.' Ludwig groaned.

'Terrible! Terrible!' he said, brokenly. 'The mess they make in the suites getting in and out on to the roof. I feel terrible! It is my holiday tomorrow.'

'But you didn't set fire to the sign,' I pointed out.

'No! No, but I was on duty,' said Ludwig, his eyes anguished. 'It caught fire when I was on duty.'

'Very inconsiderate of it,' I said, soothingly. 'But it didn't burn the hotel down, so you're all right. Come and have a drink and calm down. Or, if you prefer it, they've got an ambulance outside.'

'No, no, thank you,' said Ludwig, refusing my offer of the ambulance quite seriously. 'I cannot leave the hotel now. I must clean up the mess.'

He met me later for a drink and he was still in a highly nervous condition.

'Have you those pills for me?' he asked, plaintively. 'With this happening now it is worse, you understand.'

'Damn!' I said. 'I forgot. But don't worry; you shall have them. What time do you leave?'

'Two o'clock,' said Ludwig, like someone stating the time of his own execution.

'I shall have lunch in the Bella Vista,' I said. 'Pop in and have a glass before you go and I'll have the pills ready.'

'Thank you,' said Ludwig. 'I feel that without them I cannot enjoy my holiday.'

The next day, I had just demolished a delicious bowl of stracciatella, followed by a piece of crumbed veal with a green salad, accompanied by an excellent bottle of chianti, when Ludwig appeared, hands twitching, dark circles under his eyes.

'Have you got them?' he asked, desperately.

'Yes,' I said, giving him a professional look. 'Now, sit down and relax for a moment. You're enough to make any woman drop her brassiere on the floor.'

I eased one of the green and black pills out of the envelope into which I had put his supply.

'Now,' I said, in my best Harley Street manner. 'You want to take one a day, no more. Do you understand? And only if you need it. OK?'

'Yes! Yes!' he said, eyeing the pill as though it were a touchstone that could turn all things to gold.

I ordered another bottle of wine and poured him a glass. He gulped it down. I poured him another.

'Now take your pill,' I said.

'Are you sure you can drive with them?' he asked.

'You can drink and drive,' I assured him. 'They've never had the slightest effect on me. I have just taken one, as a matter of fact.'

'Good,' he said, swallowing the pill. 'But I must drive a lot, you see, and so it is important.'

'Quite,' I said. 'But you're safe. They won't affect you.'

After another glass of wine, he rose to his feet and wrung my hand.

'I am so glad we met,' he said.

'So am I,' I said. 'Come over and see me some time. Bring Penny. I don't mind if she drops her brassiere on the floor.'

'You are joking,' he said, with pride. 'I can tell now when you joke.'

'Well, have a good holiday,' I said, and watched him twitch his way down to his Mercedes and his brief freedom from the cares of the hotel.

I finished the wine and then went to the cinema.

It was a film I had long wanted to see and I was greatly looking forward to it. I paid my admission and chose my seat with care. The cinema darkened and the titles of the film appeared on the screen – then I knew nothing more until, three quarters of an hour later, I was woken by a man in the seat behind me shaking my shoulder and asking me not to snore so loudly as he couldn't hear the dialogue. I leapt to my feet in astonishment. I had never fallen asleep in the cinema in my life. It must have been that damned pill, plus the wine, I thought.

Then I remembered Ludwig and went cold.

My God! He'll be bowling along on his way to meet Penny and he'll suddenly fall into a deep sleep behind the wheel of his Mercedes, I thought. I visualized the crumpled, blood-stained wreckage wrapped round a tree. Hopefully, I wondered if perhaps he hadn't started yet. I fled from the cinema like one possessed, and burst into the garage, doubtless looking as distraught and wild-eyed as Ludwig did in an emergency.

'Mr Dietrich – has he gone?' I asked the attendant.

'Yes, sir, he left nearly an hour ago,' he said.

I must confess, I had a very uncomfortable three days before I received a postcard from Calais which eased my mind. It said: 'Have met Penny and am starting tomorrow for a happy holiday.' It was signed: 'Your filthy Hun, Ludwig.'

Somewhere there is, I believe, a saying about having the last laugh, but I am sure that Ludwig had never heard of it.

The Jury

The river steamer *Dolores* broke down – as river steamers are wont to do – midway between her point of departure and her destination at Meriada, a small township of some two thousand souls on the banks of the Parana River. There seemed no justification for this misdemeanour for here the river was wide, deep, placid and with a good current that was hastening us on our way. I was annoyed for I had in the hold, among other things, two jaguars, twenty monkeys and an assortment of some thirty birds and reptiles. I had calculated my food supply for a five-day journey and if we were delayed too long my supplies would run out. My two jaguars, though tame as kittens, lived to eat and their agonized screams of rage and frustration if their demand for three square meals a day was not met were a blood-curdling cacophony that had to be heard to be believed.

I went to see the captain. He was a squat, dark-skinned little man with a heavy black moustache and eyebrows, a mass of curly hair, very white teeth, and he smelt overpoweringly of Parma violets.

'Capitano,' I said. 'I am sorry to worry you, but have you any idea how long we will remain here? I am worried about food for my animals.'

He gave one of those wide, enormously expressive Latin shrugs and raised his eyes heavenwards.

'Señor, I cannot tell you,' he said. 'The part of the Hico de Puta engine which is broken they *say* that it may be mended at a forge in town, but I doubt it. If it cannot be mended we must send back for the part from our last port of call.'

'Has someone phoned back for one?' I enquired.

'No,' said the captain, shrugging. 'The telephones are out of order. They cannot mend them until tomorrow, they say.'

'Well, I'm going into town to get some more food for my bichos. Don't leave without me, will you?'

He laughed.

'No fear of that, señor,' he said. 'Look, I'll send a couple of the Indios with you to carry. They have nothing to do at the moment.'

So I and my two Indians padded off along the road to the centre of town where I knew, inevitably, the market lay. These were real Paraguayan Indians, small of stature, copper skinned, with straight soot-black hair and eyes like blackberries. Presently, loaded down with avocados, bananas, oranges, pineapples, four legs of goat meat and fourteen live chickens, we made our way back to the *Dolores*. I stored my comestibles, ignored the jaguars' efforts to get me to play with them, and went back on deck. Here I was surprised to find a gentleman occupying one of the few dilapidated deck-chairs provided for the delight of passengers. Most of them were so frayed you feared to sit in them, most so rotten they collapsed if you touched them. This gentleman had, however, found one of the rare ones that supported weight. He now rose, swept off his enormous straw hat and held out his hand.

'My dear sir,' he said in perfect English, 'may I welcome you to Meriada, though, of course, this delay must be irritating for you. My name is Menton, James Menton, and you, I believe, are Mr Durrell?' I admitted this fact while I stared at him.

His hair, brown flecked with grey, stretched down his back almost to his buttocks and was neatly plaited and the ends kept under control by a small leather lariat with a blue stone in it. His beard, moustache and eyebrows were immense and untouched by scissors as far as I could judge, though scrupulously clean. He had huge green eyes which flicked from side to side and his body twitched in an odd disjointed way, giving him somewhat the aspect of a slender, agitated animal hiding in a bush.

'Now my dear fellow,' he continued, 'the reason I came a-running when I heard you were on board was to invite you to stay with me. I know what these river steamers are like, stink to high heaven, oily, nasty, uncomfortable and serving you food that looks as though it has been refused at the local pigsty. You must admit it, eh?'

I had to admit it. The *Dolores* was all and more than he described.

'Now,' he continued, pointing, 'just through the trees there is my house. Wonderful veranda, fans – the lovely old sort that look like windmills in Holland – screened in, so no bugs, one ancient German maid who cooks like a dream and, my dear fellow, the most comfortable hammocks from Guinea, imported them myself. Give you the most wonderful sleep in the world, I do assure you.'

'You make it sound irresistible,' I said, smiling.

'But, I must confess to you,' he said, holding up a hand that trembled and twitched, 'my wish to have you stay with me is certainly a selfish one. You see, one gets so little company here – I mean real company. People don't come here to stay. It gets lonely.'

I looked at the ramshackle dock, the oily water full of beer cans and more sordid detritus, the starved dogs foraging along the shoreline. I had already seen the dilapidated township and its tatterdemalion inhabitants.

'No, I can see it is hardly a tourist spot,' I said, 'so I will be glad to take you up on your offer, Mr Menton.'

'Oh, James, please,' he exclaimed.

'But I will have to be back here at five to feed my animals.'

'Your animals?' he queried.

'Yes, I collect animals for zoos in Europe. I have a whole host of them in the hold.'

'How extraordinary— What a curious occupation,' he exclaimed delightedly. In view of what he was to vouchsafe to me later, on looking back I found this odd.

'I'll go and get my things together,' I said. 'Won't be a moment.'

'I wonder,' he said, urgently, 'I am really ashamed to ask it, but you haven't got any *whisky* about you? You see, I've stupidly run out and so has the local store and we won't get any more until the supply ship comes in next week. I know it's an awful imposition . . .' his voice trailed away.

'Not at all,' I said. 'As a matter of fact I have discovered here, in Paraguay of all places, a rather good Scotch that goes under the unlikely name of "Dandy Dinmont". It's really very smooth and drinkable. I was taking six crates back to Argentina for friends because that stuff they dish out in Buenos Aires called "Old Smuggler" is only fit to remove the rust from ancient cars. I'll get a crate of Dandy and you can try it.'

'Too kind, really kind. I'll get a couple of Indians to help you carry your things,' he said, and he twitched even more behind his hairy bush as he sped away disjointedly.

I got together the few things I thought necessary for my sojourn with James Menton and pulled out from under my bunk one crate of the six Dandy Dinmonts and handed it over to the two smiling Indians who waited outside my minuscule and grubby cabin. As soon as they appeared on deck, James flung himself into a flurry of twitches. It was obvious that his main concern was for the whisky and he occasionally referred to the señor's crate as though it were a chalice full of holy water that must not under any circumstances be spilt. To the sure-footed, lithe, competent Indian who carried the divine nectar on his shoulder, he gave constant instructions as we wended our way along the river bank to his house.

'Now watch that root. Now here's a slippery bit coming. Watch that branch – now mind that log . . .' he went on twitching and instructing until we climbed up the wooden steps to his spacious veranda and the crate of whisky was safely installed on the table.

His house was a faded two-storey clapboard one, with huge windows and shutters and the wide veranda running right round the lower floor of the building. To allow for the vagaries of the Parana River's moods, the whole house was perched upon massive wooden piles some ten feet above the ground. The garden – if you could describe this wilderness in such grandiose terms – was full of orange, avocado, mango and loquat trees, through which you could see stretches of the river sliding and glinting along.

'Now,' said James, his voice shaking as much as his hands, 'a little libation – that's to say with your permission. A small toast to welcome you here.'

He undid the crate and pulled out a bottle and his hands shook so much that I thought he would drop it. Casually, I took it from his frantically clutching hands.

'It's curious,' I said, 'that they even have a picture of a Dandy Dinmont on the label. I wonder why they chose such an obscure breed of dog?'

I placed the bottle safely on the table and he gazed at it as if hypnotized. Suddenly he jerked as if awakening.

'Anna,' he shouted, 'Anna, bring glasses.'

There was a muttered response from the back of the house and presently Anna appeared bearing a tray with two large tumblers on it. She was a squat woman, with grey hair done in a bun speared by a forest of hair-pins. She could have been forty or ninety and her grim face and cold eyes suggested she might have enjoyed herself for a period in control of one of the less pleasant concentration camps. She eyed the whisky bottle and the crate from which it had emerged.

'Remember what Herr Doktor is saying,' she said, somewhat ominously.

'Now, now, Anna,' said James tersely, 'Mr Durrell does not want to hear all our parochial tittle-tattle.'

She grunted and went off into the house. James got the screw cap off the bottle and, with a fine feat of juggling during which I thought at one point he was going to smash both glasses with the neck of the bottle, he poured a modest tot for me and nearly a full glass for himself. I noticed, with that faint shock you get when you see people using the 'wrong' hand for writing or pouring drinks, that he was left-handed.

'Never take soda,' he explained, apologetically, 'spoils the taste. Well, here's how and welcome.'

I had barely got my glass to my lips when his was empty, its contents disappearing in three huge swallows. He twitched his way to a long chair and fell into it shuddering. One could see the whisky unravelling his nerves as one would unravel an old piece of knitting.

'Always say first sundowner is best of day,' he said through chattering teeth, attempting to smile.

'So do I,' I agreed, forbearing to point out that it was just five and the sun had not yet set. 'I think I'll just go and feed my animals and tuck them in for the night, then I'm all free.'

'Good, good,' he said, vaguely, but he was not looking at me. His gaze was fastened on the bottle.

My creatures, each in its own way, abused me, reviled me, slandered me and condemned me out of hand for being five minutes late with their food. But gradually their ferocious criticism of my callousness died away to give place to the contented champing of jaws, the slushing of fruit and the cracking of nuts.

As I walked back to the house along the river bank admiring the scissortails acting up to their names, their long tail feathers crisscrossing as they dipped and wheeled after insects, on the opposite bank of the river I could see a huge storm boiling into being. Immense cumulus clouds were shouldering their way towards us, black, purple and grey-blue as a Persian cat, with yellow and white claws of lightning flashing through them. Dimly one could hear the snarl of the storm thunder as it stalked us down.

'I say, Mr Durrell, just a minute,' a voice shouted.

Hurrying towards me was a short, dumpy little man with a grizzled moustache, a plump face and gimlet-like brown eyes. He was totally bald. He was wearing a crumpled, rather grubby linen suit and he carried a black bag. From one pocket trailed part of a stethoscope, like a piece of intestine. It took no deductive genius to place him as a doctor.

'Dr Larkin,' he said, as he shook my hand. 'I'm doctor for the Tannin Company officially, but I do a little moonlighting for some of the poor bloody Indians. Treat them like dirt, you know, these bloody Paraguayans with their airs and graces, just because they got a drop or two of Spanish blood in their lazy veins. Indians salt of the earth. Sorry to delay you, just wanted to ask how James is.

Haven't seen him for a day or two, been too busy. Is he keeping pretty fit, eh?'

'Well,' I said judiciously, 'if you call drinking a tumblerful of Scotch in thirty seconds flat keeping fit . . .'

'Dammit to hell,' he exploded, 'who gave him the bloody stuff? I've told everyone here not to give him a drop, not a drop. I was just getting him nicely dried out, too.'

'I'm afraid I'm the culprit,' I said, contritely. 'I had no idea he was an alcoholic and when he asked me to stay he mentioned he'd run out of Scotch, and I had some I was taking down to Buenos Aires so I gave him a crate.'

'God! A crate!' exclaimed Larkin. 'After his dry-out, who knows what he'll be seeing. It was worse than pink elephants, I can tell you, when I took him over.'

'I'm terribly sorry,' I said.

'Not your fault. Natural, kindly action. But look here, see if you can get the rest of the stuff – or some of it – away from him. I warn you, they're as cunning as weasels when they get to that stage. Well, no sense in my coming along. Red rag to a bull. Look, here's my card. If things get difficult, phone me. He has terrible hallucinations, d'you see, but take no notice. He'll probably tell you a lot of guff – play him along – pretend to believe him. I'll try and get over in the morning, all right?'

'Fine, and I'm sorry I mucked up your AA,' I said.

He smiled briefly.

'Can't save 'em all,' he said, and stumped off.

When I returned to the house James was well away, the bottle empty except for a finger of whisky lurking at the bottom. Beside him on the table was an ancient wind-up gramophone and a pile of old records. In view of what happened later, it was macabrely apposite that he was playing the Mills Brothers singing 'Miss Otis Regrets'.

'My dear fellow,' he said, hastily pouring the remains of the whisky into his glass, 'my dear fellow, finished your chores, what? Time for a sundowner – I'll bet you've earned it, eh? This bottle appears to be empty, so we'd better open another, eh? That's the spirit.' His hands were now quite steady as he poured out two normal drinks, one for himself and one for me.

As the evening wore on, however, he got drunker and drunker. He scarcely touched the excellent dinner that Anna had prepared for us but sat slouched silently at the end of the table clutching his glass, whisky bottle within easy reach.

'Tell me,' I said, more to make conversation than anything else, 'how did you come by this handsome house?'

'House?' he asked. 'This one? Inherited it. My aunt. This house and an allowance providing I never set foot in Merrie England again. She didn't like my reputation, d'you see? Not that I liked it much myself at that time.'

He took a gulp of whisky.

'What d'you think my vocation was? Go on, guess,' he said, a cunning glint in his green eyes.

'Well,' I said, 'it's hard to tell. You're obviously well educated. Were you something in the City, perhaps, or maybe a teacher, or maybe in the Civil Service?'

'Well, you're nearly right,' he said, and gave a drunken hoot of laughter. 'I *was* in Government service, quite right. But I was also a teacher. Special sort of teacher. Can you guess?'

'I have no idea,' I said. 'There are so many variations in the academic world.'

'Academic world! I like that. No, my boy, I taught killing. Professional killing,' he said, and filled his glass almost to the brim.

'You mean you taught commandos or marines or something of that sort?' I asked, but I was beginning to get a decidedly creepy feeling about him and longed to be safely back on board ship in my smelly little cabin.

'Marines be damned,' he said, gulping at his drink. 'No, my dear fellow, I taught hanging.'

He suddenly jerked his head to one side in a horribly realistic impression of a hanged man.

'Yes, that's what I taught. Taught 'em to tie the knot that works wonders. The knot that is the answer to everything. The knot that sends you swiftly to eternity. The knot that causes you less trouble than the wedding knot.'

'You mean you were a public hangman?' I asked incredulously.

'No,' he said, 'I was a *travelling* hangman. Of course, I had my basic training in England. Didn't have much to do except watch and learn. There's a real art to it, you know, cracking a neck just right, so they don't suffer, d'you see? Mathematics enters into it too, you know, getting them to stand on the trap so they'll drop straight, judging height and weight and thickness of neck. It's an art, as I say.' He stopped and shuddered violently and drained his glass.

'The trouble is the bastards don't stay dead,' he said, his voice breaking. 'They won't stay away. Why can't they remain where they are and stop coming back and causing trouble? They were condemned, God dammit.'

His green eyes welled with tears which trickled out into his moustache and beard and were absorbed as snowflakes on a tundra.

'Why can't they leave me alone?' he asked me desperately. 'I only did my job.'

'You mean you dream about them?' I asked.

'*Dream* about them? Hell, no. If I *dreamt* about them Doc Larkin's got something that sends you out like a light and you don't bloody dream. I wish I *did* dream about 'em. Doc could cure that.'

'You mean you – er – see them?' I asked. I hesitated to use the term hallucination for fear he would take offence.

'Let me tell you how it is. As I said, I did my basic training tail end of the war. Quite a few we topped then and so I got the hang of it. Ha! Sorry, slipped out, wasn't intended as a joke. Well, the war ended and of course there were dozens that needed topping and in most of the countries – you know, like New Guinea, parts of Africa, Malaya, even Brisbane in Australia – they didn't have hangmen, I mean proper hangmen that knew the art d'you see? So they used to send me out and I'd top 'em in bunches because they'd save 'em up. But while I was out there I'd teach one or two of the local guys how to do it. I was a sort of travelling professor in death.'

He gave a small, hiccoughing gulp of laughter and some more tears welled out and trickled down to become invisible in his moustache. He refilled his glass and checked the level of the Scotch in the bottle.

'Then I was sent out to hang a man in a place in Malaya. Owing to overcrowding in the township prison, he'd been moved to a village prison twenty-five miles away. You know the sort of thing, six mud cells, a sergeant and two lesser ranks in control. The sergeant was all right but slovenly. The lesser ranks were, as usual, vacant-faced and even more vacant-minded. Finally I got the scaffold up and working to my liking. Then came the day of the execution. I got up at dawn, tested the scaffold and then found the sergeant drunk and drugged out of his mind in bed with a sixteen-year-old girl in a similar state. I routed out the two underlings who were, thank God, sober. They brought the prisoner to the scaffold and I prepared him. Then, as usual, I asked him if he had anything to say. He, of course, spoke only Malay, but one of the underlings translated in primitive English. He said that the man said he was guilty of no crime. Most of them say that of course, so I put the hood on and away he went. Quick and clean.'

He lowered his head on to his arms for a moment and his shoulders shook. He lifted his tear-stained face and stared at me.

'I had hanged the wrong man,' he said.

'Dear God!' I exclaimed, horrified. 'What did you do?'

'What could I do?' he asked. 'I had seen the man through the Judas window in the town jail. I'd been given his weight and height, of course, and I had assessed the thickness of the neck, the shape and balance of the head. All important stuff. But, bloody hell, I can't tell one heathen from another, never could. And the bloody sergeant was too drugged and drunk to guide me, and his underlings too stupid.'

'But didn't he struggle or anything?'

'No, they seem to take death very calmly in those parts.'

He poured himself another tumblerful of Scotch. I wondered how many bottles were left.

'You can imagine the furore it caused when it leaked out. World headlines. "Horrific Hangman". "The Man Who Kills for Fun". "The Brutal Executioner". "The Careless Killer". That sort of thing. Surprised you didn't see it.'

'I was in Africa, a bit remote,' I said, not adding that I was most likely in a village forty miles from the nearest road and *The Times* was not delivered each morning.

'Well that was the end of me. Of course, they had an official enquiry and sort of implied I was guilty of negligence. They said I should have waited until the sergeant surfaced. But how could I? I had a plane to catch and another job to do. I couldn't keep the other poor chaps hanging around now, could I?' He seemed unconscious of what he had said.

'So they gave me the golden bum's rush. My aunt, a pillar of the Church, was horrified, of course, and so she fixed me up financially and sent me out here. It was beginning then but I thought, dammit, Paraguay's so far they can't follow me there.'

'Who couldn't follow you?' I asked, puzzled.

He looked at me and his eye filled with tears again.

'The faces,' he sobbed. 'Their bloody faces.'

I waited until he got control of himself.

'You see, it started one day when I was shaving. I noticed that one side of my face was a sort of blur – out of focus, sort of thing. Well, I went to the quack and he sent me to an eye specialist. They couldn't find a thing wrong. But the blur went on and got worse. My whole face was out of focus. I could only just see to shave. Then, suddenly one day, I looked in the mirror and it wasn't my face staring at me, it was the face of O'Mara, the first man I'd hanged – up country in Nigeria somewhere – cut his wife to bits with a knife. Well, I was so surprised I just stared at the mirror and then O'Mara grinned at me. He jerked his head one side, lolled his tongue, then straightened up, grinned at me again, winked and vanished. I thought it was the whisky. You may have noticed I like a drop or two. So I started to shave and the next minute my face blurred over and there was the face of Jenkins. God, how he glared at me. I dropped the razor with fright. Then he was gone and it was Yu Ling, and then Thomson, and then Ranjit Singh and so on and so on, twelve of 'em. I remember vomiting into the bath and shaking all over as if I had a dose of malaria. I knew I couldn't tell my doc about it – he'd have had me in a padded cell before you could say Jack Robinson. I thought it might be the mirror, so I went out and bought another. But by the next morning they'd found it. I bought another one – same thing. I thought it might be the size or the shape of it. I spent a fortune on mirrors, but it was no good, they got their faces on every one, every bloody one. That's why I grow all this,' he said, fingering his face, 'this stupid beard.'

'But surely a barber . . .' I began.

'No,' he said, 'first man I adjusted the rope round, my fingers brushed his neck. Sort of warm, soft, velvety, you know. I remember thinking: "In thirty seconds this neck's going to be broken and in a few hours it won't be warm and velvety, it'll feel like cold mutton." It sort of shook me up, you know. Upset me more than a little. So I don't like people messing around my throat or neck. Makes me uncomfortable. Silly, really. But there it is. So, no barbers. D'you believe me – about the mirrors, I mean?'

'Yes, of course,' I said, trying to put what conviction I could into my voice. 'You obviously saw something that scared you.'

He filled his glass and glanced at his watch.

'Got a board meeting tonight to settle it once and for all. Can't be late for it. Must keep sober. They're cunning as Machiavelli. But we've just got time. Come, let me show you something.'

Carrying his glass as carefully as if it were a life support system, he led me down a corridor where there were two huge double doors. These he unlocked, threw them open and switched on a blaze from a giant glittering chandelier in the centre of the room. It was a long room, perhaps some forty feet by twenty and down its length ran a wide, beautifully polished rosewood table. Along its sides twelve chairs were arranged, six to a side, and at the end of the table stood the thirteenth chair, a heavily carved ornate piece of furniture with massive arms. The whole end wall was covered by a gigantic mirror in a gold frame, which reflected the table, the chairs and the chandelier above them. It was an impressive room but the most amazing thing about it was the walls on which hung a multitude of mirrors of every shape, size and colour, ranging from tall pier glasses to round bathroom mirrors, to tiny mirrors from ladies' compacts. They were round, oval, square, even triangular. Some had ornate frames, others cheap wooden ones, others stark chromium surrounds.

The only thing they had in common was that they were each spiked to the wall by a pointed iron peg, which drove straight through the centre of the mirror, splintering it.

'D'you see?' said James, swaying slightly and waving at the mirrors. 'Tried 'em all. But they got into 'em, like rats into a hayrick. There's about a thousand years of bad luck pinned to these walls if you're superstitious. Ha! I got my bad luck before I broke 'em.'

He gazed with surprise at his empty glass and glanced at his watch.

'Let's go and have another drink,' he said. 'There's plenty of time.'

I noticed then, with a tingle of apprehension, that in front of each neatly pushed-in chair, except the thirteenth, was a printed place card. I had just time to read some before he switched the light off: O'Mara, Ranjit Singh, Jenkins, all the hanged men he had mentioned. He had said a board meeting, but it looked more like a jury room to me – a jury of twelve dead men. I shivered and hoped he would not ask me to attend as an observer.

He carefully locked the big double doors and we made our way out on to the veranda. The storm was crouched directly above us now and was endeavouring to devour the house, shaking it with thunder, running its talons of lightning along the steel guttering producing showers of sparks, salivating a downpour of rain, whose noise on the roof almost obliterated the cackling of the frogs. We had to shout to make ourselves heard.

'It'll pass,' James said, filling our glasses, 'they always do.'

But the storm did not want to pass. It remained above us, anchored to us, as though it knew something uncanny was going to happen and wanted to play its part. It sat over us as a cat squats over a half-dead mouse, waiting for movement.

James looked at his watch.

'Must go now, my dear fellow,' he shouted. 'Apologies, but this is an important meeting. You know your room, don't you? Well, if we make too much row just bang on the floor. I doubt if you'll hear us, though, with all this racket going on.'

He rose, apparently perfectly sober, as urbane as any host I had ever stayed with.

'Sorry about this,' he said, 'but it's important, you know, to get things clear.'

'I quite understand,' I said.

So as he made his way to the weird room with its multitude of broken mirrors, I made my way upstairs to my room with the gigantic Guyanese hammock hanging down its length. Folded over it was a vicuña wool blanket, soft and light as a spider's web, warm as a bonfire. I undressed, wrapped myself in it and made my way out cautiously to the head of the stairs and squatted down. The thunder made another attempt to disembowel the house, savaging it with lightning, and then all was silent for a brief while and I heard James Menton's voice:

'But you must realize I was a public servant, a servant of the crown. I didn't condemn you, Jenkins, it was the judge and jury . . . why don't you go and plague them . . . because I killed you? But don't you see, I was paid to kill you – you were guilty . . . Oh, yes you were, dammit, her body in the boot of your car – knife all covered with your fingerprints – her blood on your clothes . . . circumstantial evidence be damned. No, I didn't tell anyone you shat yourself just before I dropped you. You don't say . . .'

There was another roar of thunder and it lasted so long I missed the rest of the exchange. Then silence returned and I heard the clink of the bottle on the glass. There was no sound of other voices, only that of Menton's.

'You know perfectly well, Yu Ling, it was an accident – I

watched you through the Judas window for half an hour, but you sat all hunched up. I couldn't see your neck was that slender. Professional hangmen don't make a habit of tearing off the head, you know. I know it was a disgrace for you . . .'

More thunder and a splintering crash as lightning hit one of the drain-pipes and it broke loose.

I sat at the head of the stairs for perhaps two hours listening to Menton arguing with the men he had hanged while thunder shook the house, until it felt as if we were like dice in a cup. At one point I crept downstairs and helped myself to a whisky and retreated to the head of the stairs again to listen to Menton.

'All right! All right!' he shouted at last. 'You can have ten minutes to, as you put it, consider your verdict. I will take ten minutes to give myself a drink and consider my verdict.'

I rose and moved back from the head of the stairs as he came out rapidly, closed the doors and then loped off down the corridor to the veranda. I wondered whether I should join him on the pretext of insomnia, but I heard him pour himself a drink and start pacing up and down, muttering to himself, and I decided against it. For the moment the storm seemed to have retreated; there was only the steady thrash of rain like fine gravel being flung at the fabric of the house, and the odd flicker of golden lightning. Suddenly, he came swiftly back down the hall, holding in one hand the inevitable tumbler of whisky. He burst through the double doors in a blaze of light and then shut them.

'Well, gentlemen, if I may call you that, have you considered your verdict?'

I leant forward to listen, and the storm that had been lying in wait leapt on the house with a clap of thunder that surpassed all the others. As it died, I heard Menton's voice.

'So *that's* your verdict is it? Well, I'll tell you what I think of you, you murderous lot. You deserved everything you got. You've got the brains of mentally retarded children. You all deserved to die and I'm damn glad to have had the job of topping you all. I'm proud, d'you hear, proud to have cleared the earth of such scum . . .'

Another clap of thunder drowned his tirade.

'Don't antagonize them, you idiot,' I found myself saying, as if his imaginary jury was flesh and blood. The thunder rumbled on and I heard no more of Menton's voice. Presently, I heard what I took to be a snore and, judging that the whisky had at last done its work and James was now asleep at the table, I went back to my hammock, but I confess I slept fitfully.

When I awoke, I went straight to James's room where his huge hammock hung like a long white pod bereft of its seeds. I went downstairs and knocked on the big double doors in the dark hall.

'James,' I called, 'it's me, Gerry. Can I come in?' There was no reply. I tried the handle and the door was locked. I leant against it and it seemed flimsy enough. Stepping back I drove my heel at the keyhole. At the second kick the doors flew open and I was momentarily blinded by the blaze from the chandelier which had been left on. I went into the room and looked down its length. Everything was reflected in the huge mirror on the end wall, the expanse of polished wood with the place cards, the chairs and then at the end, where the thirteenth chair should have been, hung the body of James Menton from the beam above. He was not a pretty sight. The big chair he must have occupied lay on its side by the table. It was clear that he had hoisted the chair up on to the table (or somebody had?), fixed the rope on the beam and then kicked the chair away (or had somebody pulled it?). He was very obviously dead, but I felt I ought to cut him down.

I went to the kitchen quarters and found a sharp knife. With an effort I hoisted the great chair back on to the table. At close quarters, James's mortal remains were even less attractive than from a distance for, apart from the overpowering stench of excretal, his nose had bled and his beard and moustache were caked in icicles of dried blood. I had to hold him close to me to support his weight as I cut the rope, with the result that we were face to face and the rancid smell of whisky almost made me vomit. As I cut through the rope and took his weight, the chair, on the smooth surface of the table, slid like a stone on ice, and it, the corpse and I crashed to the ground. Unfortunately, I landed on top of James and my weight made him void more excrement with a hideous bubbling sound and, at the same time, the slight loosening of the noose round the neck released an expulsion of fetid breath into my face. I scrambled to my feet, went out into the kitchen and was violently sick.

I decided the best thing to do was to phone Doctor Larkin. In spite of the fact that it was only just dawn, he answered at the second ring.

'Si, Doctorio Larkin,' he said, 'quien habla?'

'It's me, Gerry Durrell,' I said.

'What's James been up to?' he asked.

'Very bad hallucinations last night, and I found him hanged this morning.'

'You mean he hanged himself?' said Larkin sharply.

'Er – yes, I suppose so. I cut him down. No doubt he's dead. The knot was under the right ear so he choked to death, rather than having a clean drop.'

'Wrong ear, eh? So much for his tales about being a hangman.'

'No, he was very drunk, and he was left-handed,' I explained, but in the back of my mind I kept thinking – 'I wonder who arranged to have him die in this most painful way?'

'Look,' said Larkin, 'you get out of there. Pack your things and get back on the *Dolores*. She's going to sail in an hour, so I hear. But don't hang about or they'll arrest you.'

'Arrest me for what, for God's sake?'

'In Paraguay, if you're a gringo, they'll arrest you for any reason at all. D'you want to spend the next year in prison while a bunch of dago lawyers argue it out?'

'No,' I said firmly.

'Well, collect your things and get on that ship. I'll be round immediately and I'll report and say I cut him down. All right?' 'All right,' I said.

'Oh, and Durrell, I suppose there's none of that Scotch left, is there?'

'Miraculously enough, two bottles.'

'Put them on the veranda table for me, if you would.'

'Is that your fee?' I enquired.

'No, it's for the Chief of Police. Goodbye.' He slammed down the receiver.

I packed my few things hastily and went downstairs and to my astonishment found a smiling Indian waiting.

'Capitano . . . ship . . . goodbye,' he said.

I handed him my bundle and gestured him to go ahead. There was just one thing I had to check on; something that had caught my eye, but I had not registered properly, I went back into the big room where poor James's bloated and disfigured body lay and I looked at the table. I realized with a faint shiver that I had not been mistaken. All of the twelve chairs with the name cards had been swivelled round to face the top end of the table, as if the people who were in them had half turned their chairs to get a better view. A better view of what? An execution?

Miss Booth-Wycherly's Clothes

I only came to know about Miss Booth-Wycherly's clothes – and the unsettling effect they had on such a remarkable cross-section of humanity, ranging from the villagers of San Sebastian, to the Little Sisters of Innocence and the croupiers of Monte Carlo – because I happened to know Miss Booth-Wycherly.

When I go down to my small house in the South of France each year to get some writing done, I always make a detour and spend a few days in Monte Carlo with two friends of mine, Jean and Melanie Schultz. Jean is a retired Swiss banker with a bandit moustache and a roguish blue eye, a man of considerable means, and Melanie is a gorgeous American girl, one of those slender girls with long dark hair and a profile that makes young men gaze with sagging jaws. I loved them both very much and it was only because of this that, when they expressed a desire to go to the Casino one night while I was staying with them, I reluctantly agreed.

I am no gambling man. I learnt at a very early age that you have to possess a certain kind of karma to gamble successfully. If I back a horse or a dog they instantly develop foot-and-mouth disease or rabies. If I back black on the roulette table red comes up with a positively Maoist malevolence. I had learnt through bitter experience that if I bet someone that the sky was blue it would instantly turn black with storm clouds. I therefore came to the conclusion that I was not designed by Nature to gamble and so I never did. My friends, however, had no such inhibitions and settled themselves down happily to bleed their bank accounts.

Left to myself, I wandered about watching the people who played, a wonderful assortment of individuals ranging from a tiny hunchback who looked like a gypsy to a svelte blonde who had walked straight out of the pages of *Vogue*, from a Negro in tails with a face as impassive as an Easter Island statue to an enormously fat man whose purple face and stertorous breathing heralded the fact that he would, in all probability, die at the table. But even amongst this extraordinary crowd Miss Booth-Wycherly stood out and caught my attention.

She was a small, fragile woman whose skin, at the throat, hung in folds and pleats like a curtain. Her face was a network of fine wrinkles like a relief map of the mouth of some great river. Her nose was prominent and arched like an eagle's beak. Her eyes were blue, a muzzy, watery blue, like faded periwinkles, and in the left one she wore a monocle tethered by a long piece of watered ribbon. Her clothes were incredible. They had obviously been designed and constructed somewhere in the very early nineteen-twenties. Her full-length dress was in crimson velvet with gold filigree buttons and long sleeves. She wore a large crimson velvet hat which was trimmed with yellow ostrich feathers and the fur of some animal that looked as though it was as yet unknown to science. This same fur was around her collar and the edges of her sleeves and the hem of her dress. Round her tortoise neck hung several long loops of multi-coloured beads and to that part of her dress that presumably concealed her bosom was pinned a large yellow satin rose. Her hands, which looked as if made out of the dead and brittle twigs of some exotic tree, were beautifully shaped and she used them gracefully as she manoeuvred her collection of chips. There was a faint touch of eye-shadow, of rouge on the cheekbones, and lipstick on her mouth, but not enough to turn her into an ancient clown. When she smiled at the croupiers, her false teeth were excellent and white. I judged her to be in her late seventies and was surprised to find later that she was eighty-two. She was, to judge by her atrocious French accent, English.

She had before her on the table a small notebook in which she carefully wrote down the numbers that came up. She had that dreaded thing called 'a system'. Most compulsive gamblers (compulsive gambling is a disease, like alcoholism) have a system to which they cling with blind faith. The fact that the system does not work is neither here nor there, it gives them comfort like a rabbit's foot and is just about as much use. They will lose nineteen out of twenty bets but the one win proves their system infallible. The compulsive gamblers, as opposed to the ordinary ones, could be picked out with ease. Fanatically they watched the tiny ball making its deadly machine-gun rattle as it spun round the wheel, and their faces became intense, predatory, as the ball slowed and clicked and finally sank to rest in a numbered hole. They would let out their breath in a long sigh, like someone at the conclusion of a beautiful piece of music, and if they had won turn triumphant, sparkling eyes and glittering smiles on the other gamblers and the impassive croupiers. If they had lost they busied themselves in writing down the numbers to improve their systems, their lips moving as if in silent prayer.

Miss Booth-Wycherly was a compulsive gambler par excellence. She wrote down copious notes, she arranged her chips in rows like guardsmen ready to attack, and tapped them constantly with her well-manicured nails. She placed her bet with the air of one who knows she's going to win, and then as the ball set off on its circular, wall-of-death travels, she screwed her monocle ever tighter into her eye and glared at the wheel as if she could hypnotize the ball into the right number. But it was not her evening and, as I watched, her small battalion of chips, her army of guardsmen, were whittled away by bad luck until at last she had none left. I wondered whether it was the lighting or my imagination that made me think that she had grown whiter and whiter with the loss of each chip, so that the rouge now stood out on her cheekbones making her look as if she had a fever.

She rose from the table with elegance and bowed to the croupier who expressionlessly bowed back. Then she made her way slowly out of the room. I followed her. When she came to the great entrance hall of marble columns she swayed suddenly and put out a hand to cling to one of them. I was luckily close to her and I went forward quickly and took her arm. The flesh, what there was of it, was soft and flabby and I could feel the bone of her arm through it seeming as brittle as a stick of charcoal. A strange smell emanated from her that puzzled me; it was not perfume, but something familiar. I couldn't put a name to it.

'Too kind,' she murmured, swaying. 'Too kind. I fear I must have tripped. So stupid of me.'

'Sit down a moment,' I said, guiding her to an ornate sofa that stood nearby. She tottered to it and then collapsed like a carelessly dropped puppet. She closed her eyes and then leaned back. The rouge and lipstick and eye-shadow now stood out like neon signs against the milk-white of her wrinkled face. Her monocle had fallen from her eye and lay on her heaving chest. I felt her pulse which, though faint, was steady. I caught a passing waiter.

'Get a brandy for madame, quickly,' I said.

The waiter took one look at the wrinkled wreckage in its crimson velvet gown and hat and sped away. He returned commendably quickly with the goblet containing a liberal measure of brandy.

'Drink some of this,' I said, sitting next to the old lady. 'It will do you good.'

She opened her eyes, groped for her monocle and then, after one or two abortive efforts, managed to wedge it into her eye.

She surveyed the brandy glass and then looked at me.

'Young man,' she said, drawing herself up indignantly, 'I never drink.'

Again, I got a whiff of the strange smell from her. It was on her breath and suddenly I realized what it was. Methylated spirits. The old lady was a lush as well as a gambler.

'Normally, madame, I would not insult you by offering you a strong drink,' I said, soothingly, 'but you seemed a trifle faint – the heat no doubt – and I felt that this, taken purely as a medicine, might do you good.'

She peered at me through her monocle, which had the ludicrous effect of making one eye appear larger than the other, then she examined the goblet of brandy.

'Well,' she said, 'if it's medicinal of course that's different. Daddy always used to say that a tot of brandy was better than all Harley Street.'

'I agree,' I said, warmly.

She took the glass from my hand and gulped it down, then coughed and produced a tiny scrap of lace and wiped her mouth with it.

'Warming,' she said, closing her eyes and leaning back. 'Most warming. Daddy was right.'

I let her sit quietly for a moment so that the brandy took hold. Presently she opened her eyes.

'Young man,' she said, her speech faintly slurred, 'you are absolutely right. It has made me feel worlds better.'

'Will you have another?' I asked.

'Well, I don't know that I should,' she said, judiciously, 'but perhaps a soupçon.'

I signalled the waiter and he brought another brandy. It disappeared with the miraculous suddenness of the first.

'Madame,' I said, 'since you are feeling somewhat fragile, may I have your permission to see you safely home?'

I was dying to know where this extraordinary relic lived during the daytime.

She opened her eyes and glared at me.

'Do I know you?' she enquired.

'Alas, no,' I said.

'Then it's a most improper suggestion,' she said. 'Most improper!'

'But not if I introduce myself,' I said, and proceeded to do so.

She inclined her head regally and held out her fragile hand.

'I am Suzanna Booth-Wycherly,' she said, in the manner of one announcing that she was Cleopatra.

'I am enchanted,' I said gravely and kissed her hand.

'At least you have some manners,' she admitted reluctantly. 'Well, you may see me home, if you please.'

Getting Miss Booth-Wycherly down the long staircase, hall and steps was quite a performance, since the two brandies had now taken firm hold and, while they had a detrimental effect on her legs, they unleashed a stream of reminiscences and for each one she had to pause while she told me the story. Three steps down the stairs she remembered how Daddy had first brought her here when Mummy died in 1904, and she described in great detail the assembled company. Women as multi-coloured as a flock of parakeets in their wonderful gowns, glittering jewels in such quantities that they would blind a pirate, the men so handsome, the women so beautiful; they didn't seem to breed beautiful women any more. Not like they did when she was a gal, when *everybody* seemed beautiful. At the foot of the stairs she remembered a particularly beautiful young man whom she had been enamoured of, who had gambled and lost and gone out and shot himself. So unnecessary, since Daddy would have lent him the money, and so thoughtless since the servants had to clean up the mess. Daddy said that you should always treat the lower classes with consideration, and you should not give your servants unnecessary work to do. She remembered halfway down the hall how King Edward had visited Monte in 1906 and how she'd been presented to him, and how he had been a true gentleman. The flood of remembrances continued down the steps, across the forecourt, and uninterruptedly during the taxi ride to one of the less salubrious parts of Monte Carlo. Here the taxi drew up at an alleyway between two tall ancient buildings with plaster peeling from the walls and faded sun-blistered shutters.

'Ah, home,' said Miss Booth-Wycherly, screwing her monocle into her eye and viewing the unsavoury alley. 'I have my apartment on the ground floor, just down there, second door on the left. So convenient.'

I extracted her from the taxi with some difficulty and, telling the driver to wait, I escorted her down the alley which smelt, in the hot night air, of cats, sewage and rotting vegetables in equal quantities. At the front door she placed her monocle in her eye and held out her hand graciously.

'You have been most kind, young man,' she said, 'most kind, and I have enjoyed conversing with you. It has been a great pleasure.'

'The pleasure, I assure you, was entirely mine,' I said truthfully. 'May I call tomorrow to make sure you have completely recovered from your fatigue?'

'I never receive before five,' she said.

'Then, if I may, I will come at five,' I suggested.

'I will be delighted to see you,' she said, inclining her head. She opened the door and manoeuvred her way through it a trifle uncertainly and the door closed behind her. I was loath to leave her for fear she might fall down and hurt herself, but with such an indomitable old lady you could hardly suggest undressing her and putting her to bed.

The next evening at five, bearing a basket of fruit and cheese together with a large bunch of flowers, I made my way to Miss Booth-Wycherly's abode. I knocked on her door and there came a storm of shrill yapping. Presently, the door was cautiously opened and Miss Booth-Wycherly peered out of the crack, her monocle glinting.

'Good evening, Miss Booth-Wycherly,' I said, 'I've come as we arranged.'

The door swung open a trifle and I could see she was wearing a fantastic lace nightdress. It was obvious that she had forgotten about me and my visit.

'Why, young man,' she said, 'I wasn't expecting you – er – quite so early.'

'I'm sorry, I thought you said five o'clock,' I said contritely.

'I did. Is it five already?' she asked. 'Dear me, how time flies, I was just having my siesta.'

'I am so sorry to have disturbed you,' I said. 'Shall I come back later?'

'No. No,' she said, smiling, at me graciously, 'if you don't mind me entertaining you in my night attire.'

'Your company would be a privilege in any attire,' I said gallantly.

She opened the door and I went in. The reek of stale methylated spirits was overpowering. Her flat consisted of one very large room which served as a bedroom and a living room and off it a minute kitchen and a tiny bathroom. At the end of the living room was a huge double bed. The weather being hot, there were only sheets upon it, and these were so dirty they seemed almost black.

The cause of this was sitting in the middle of the bed – a dachs-hund, with a huge ox shin-bone, covered with blood and sawdust, lying on the sheets between its paws. When it saw me looking, it growled malevolently at me. The walls on each side and above the bed were almost obliterated under a mass of ancient yellowing photographs in gilt frames. One wall of the room was occupied by two huge oak cupboards and between them a rack, like a large bookcase, on which reposed an extraordinary collection of shoes, each carefully treed. There must have been some thirty or forty pairs, ranging from brogues to sequined dance slippers. Along the other wall, piled almost to the ceiling, was a series of large leather trunks (the sort they used to call steamer trunks in the old days), each shaped like the traditional pirate's treasure chest with a rounded lid and emblazoned with the magic words, BOOTH-WYCHERLY. There was just enough room among all this clutter for a small table and three wicker chairs.

'I thought the fruit and cheese looked so good, I simply had to bring you some,' I said. 'And, of course, flowers for my hostess.'

She took the bunch of flowers in her fragile arms and to my embarrassment her eyes suddenly filled with tears.

'It's been a long time since I was given flowers,' she said.

'That's because you're too much of a recluse,' I pointed out. 'If you got out and about more, you'd have queues of men outside your door with floral offerings. I wouldn't get a look in then.'

She looked at me for a moment and then she chuckled pleasedly.

'You're what Daddy would have called a card,' she said. 'You know how to flatter an old woman.'

'Nonsense,' I said, briskly. 'You're not a day over fifty. I refuse to believe anything else.'

She chuckled again.

'It's a long time since anyone was *gallant* with me,' she said. 'A very long time. I enjoy it. I think I'm going to like you, young man.'

'I'm glad,' I answered truthfully, 'for I know that I like you.'

From that moment on, I became Miss Booth-Wycherly's con-fidant and friend. She had no relatives and no other friends; those few acquaintances she had either thought her touched, or had not the time or the interest to listen to her fund of anecdotes. But to me it was fascinating to hear her talk so vividly and so poignantly of a bygone age, an age when the British so arrogantly bestrode the earth and when the world maps were predominantly pink to show it. A world unshakeable in its solidarity and its elegance, with an endless supply of good things for those with the wealth; a world where the lower classes knew their place and a good cook was paid thirty pounds a year and had a day off a month. Miss Booth-Wycherly recaptured those far off, apparently perpetually sunlit, days for me and it was as fascinating as talking to a dinosaur. I used to visit her whenever I could, braving the assaults of the dachshund Lulu (who regularly bit me in the ankle), taking her gifts of fruit and cheese and chocolates, of which she was inordinately fond. Gradually I weaned her off methylated spirits on to brandy which I felt – if she must drink – was better for her. It certainly took less brandy to give her the desired effect. She took the brandy, of course, for purely medicinal reasons to begin with, but later she would quite blatantly suggest that we had a tot. The difficulty at first was to get her to accept the brandy, and I found the only way I could do it was to play cards with her, using the bottle as a stake. If she won, she had the bottle; if I won, we opened the bottle to celebrate and I forgot it when I left. It was during the last of these card sessions before I left France that she told me she was a Catholic.

'A very bad one, I'm afraid,' she confessed. 'I haven't been to Mass for years and years. You see, I didn't really feel I could, for I'm such a bad woman in so many ways.'

'Surely not,' I protested. 'You seem the essence of goodness to me.'

'No, no,' she said. 'You don't know all about me, young man. I've done some very wicked things in my time.'

She looked round the room furtively, to make sure we were alone, if you discounted Lulu, who sat on the bed, busily demolishing what appeared to be half a sheep.

'I was once a married man's mistress,' said Miss Booth-

Wycherly unexpectedly, and sat back to see how I would take the news.

'Bravo!' I said, imperturbably. 'I bet you made him very happy, lucky devil.'

'I did!' she said. 'Oh yes I *did*.'

'Well, there you are then. You gave happiness.'

'Yes, but immorally,' she pointed out.

'Happiness is happiness. I don't think it has anything to do with morals,' I said.

'I became pregnant by him,' she said, and took a hasty sip of brandy to recover her nerve after this revelation.

'It sometimes unfortunately happens,' I said guardedly.

'Then I did this terrible thing, a mortal sin,' she whispered. 'I had an abortion.'

I was not quite sure what to say to this, so I remained silent.

She took my silence to mean that I disapproved of her action.

'But I *had* to,' she said. 'Oh, I know people have abortions now like shelling peas, and think nothing of it. And they have illegitimate children like chickens laying eggs and it's no stigma. But when I was a gal, to have an affair with a *married man* was bad enough, but to have an abortion or an illegitimate child was *unthinkable*.'

'But didn't the Church help you?' I asked. 'I thought in moments of stress like that . . .'

'No,' interrupted Miss Booth-Wycherly. 'At the church we used to frequent we had a particularly obnoxious priest. I was very upset and at my wits' end, as you may imagine, and all he did was to compare me to the whore of Babylon.'

A tear trickled out from behind her monocle and rolled down her cheek.

'So I gave up going to church,' she said, sniffing defiantly. 'I considered they had let me down.'

'Well, I don't think that makes you irretrievably damned,' I pointed out. 'There are many worse people in the world.'

'If I wasn't financially on a tight rein,' she said, 'I would have very much liked to have helped the Church, but I'm afraid I couldn't have done anything very much. But now, after that, oh, no, never.' She had another sip of brandy. 'But I *would* like to help something like the orphanage in San Sebastian. I think the Little Sisters of Innocence do such marvellous work. *They* don't care if the children are – well, you know – illegitimate. I visited them once with Henri, he was my lover, and we were most impressed. They are good – not like those priests.'

'San Sebastian is that small village just over the border in France, isn't it?' I asked.

'Yes,' she said, 'such a pretty little mountain village.'

'Next year, when I come down, would you like me to drive you out there to visit them?' I asked.

'Oh, that would be *lovely*,' she said, radiant. 'How exciting. Something nice to look forward to.'

'It's a date,' I said, shuffling the cards. 'And now let's see who is going to win this absolutely untouched bottle of medicinal brandy.'

We played for a time and she won the brandy.

She also thought of a way to help the orphanage at San Sebastian. Yet, had she known the alarm and consternation it was going to cause, I doubt whether she would have done it – though the end result was all that she could have desired.

I returned the following year and, as usual, paid my annual visit to Jean and Melanie. After the exuberance of their greeting had died down and we were sitting having a drink, I raised my glass and toasted Melanie.

'You are,' I said, 'the best hostess in the world and the most beautiful woman in Monte Carlo.'

She inclined her lovely head, smiling.

'However,' I continued, 'lest you set too great a store by my remarks I must confess to you that my heart is lost to another. So I must leave you briefly and purchase fruit, cheese, brandy and flowers and make my way hot-foot to my loved one, the delicious, the incomparable Miss Booth-Wycherly.'

'Good God!' said Jean, startled.

'Oh, Gerry,' said Melanie in distress. 'Didn't you get our letter?'

'Letter? What letter?' I asked with an awful premonition.

'Miss Booth-Wycherly is dead, Gerry,' said Jean heavily. 'I'm sorry, we wrote at once, knowing how fond you were of her.'

'Tell me,' I said.

It appeared that Miss Booth-Wycherly had made a tiny killing at the Casino and on returning to her flat had celebrated. Then she unwisely decided to take a bath. She had slipped and, in falling, both her fragile thigh bones had snapped like sticks of celery. She lay in the bath all night while the water turned stone cold. Early in the morning a passer-by heard her faint cries for help and broke the door down. Indomitable to the last, she was still coherent enough to give the rescuer Jean and Melanie's telephone number, for I had spoken highly of them and she had no other friends. Jean had gone down immediately and taken her to hospital.

'She was magnificent, Gerry,' said Jean. 'She knew she was dying, but she was determined not to do so until she was ready. She said to the doctor who wanted to give her morphine, "Take that stuff away, young man. I've never taken drugs in my life, and I don't intend to become a drug addict now." Then she insisted on making a will. She had nothing really to leave except her bits of furniture and her clothes, but they all went to the orphanage at San Sebastian.' Jean paused and blew his nose. 'She was sinking fast, but she remained clear-headed. She said she wished you had been there, Gerry. She said that you were her special friend. She said to apologize to you for the fact that she would not be able to accompany you on your trip to the orphanage.'

'Did you get her a priest?' I asked.

'I offered, but she refused,' said Jean. 'She said she had no time for the Church. She became unconscious for a bit and then, a moment or so before she died, she suddenly regained consciousness – you know the way people sometimes do? And she put her monocle in her eye and glared at me, positively *glared*. Then she said a very peculiar thing.'

I waited patiently while he sipped his drink.

'She said, "They'll get nothing from me. Whore of Babylon, indeed! I'm a Booth-Wycherly. *I'll* show them." And then her monocle fell out of her eye and she died. Have you any idea what she meant, Gerry?' Jean asked, frowning at me.

'I think so,' I said. 'She once committed a youthful indiscretion, and her local priest, instead of helping her, said she had behaved like a whore of Babylon. She never went to church after that. I think perhaps she didn't somehow, at the end, connect the orphanage with the Church, and by leaving all her things to the orphanage she thought she was doing the priests in the eye. I suppose she thought it would create a sensation, poor old thing, and that the Church would be furious at having lost her clothes.'

'But that's just it,' Melanie cried. 'It *did* create a sensation, the most *awful* sensation. We told you in our letter.'

'Tell me,' I said.

'No, don't tell him, darling,' Jean said. 'We'll just take him to the Casino tonight.'

'I don't *want* to go to the Casino,' I said irritably, for I had not recovered from my sadness at Miss Booth-Wycherly's death. 'It won't be the same without her.'

'For the sake of her memory you must come. I will show you something and you will laugh and know that everything is all right,' said Jean.

He seemed serious, but there was a twinkle in his eye.

'He's right, Gerry dear,' said Melanie. '*Please* come.'

'All right,' I said reluctantly. 'Take me and show me, but it had better be good.'

It was.

When we got to the Casino we entered the gaming rooms and Jean said, 'Just look around and tell me what you see.'

I gazed round the tables thoughtfully. The blackjack had its usual customers including the gypsy dwarf who, to judge by his demeanour, had just made a good killing. At the chemin de fer table I spotted several old friends, including my Easter Island statue, as impassive as ever. Then I looked at the baccarat table. There was a dense crowd around it and it was obvious that someone was having an extraordinary run of luck. The crowd parted for a moment and my stomach turned over. For one awful second

I saw there, leaning forward across the table to place her bet, Miss Booth-Wycherly, wearing the same crimson velvet hat and dress she had been wearing when I first encountered her. Then she turned her head and I could see that it was not Miss Booth-Wycherly but a much younger woman in her mid-twenties, with a lovely face and large innocent blue eyes like a Persian kitten. She looked round smiling and spoke to the handsome youth who stood behind her chair. He gazed down at her adoringly and nodded vigorous agreement to whatever she said. Whoever this girl was, she was wearing Miss Booth-Wycherly's clothes and my irritation bubbled up into anger. As the wheel spun the crowd closed in and hid her from view.

'Who the *hell's* that?' I demanded. 'And what the devil's she doing in Miss Booth-Wycherty's clothes?'

'Hush,' said Jean. 'Not so loud. It's all right, Gerry.'

'But who is this bloody body-snatcher?' I asked, exasperated.

'That,' said Jean, watching me, 'is Sister Claire.'

'Sister Claire?' I echoed.

'*Sister* Claire,' repeated Melanie.

'You mean she's a nun?' I asked incredulously. 'A nun in those clothes, gambling? You must be out of your mind.'

'No, it's quite true, Gerry,' said Jean, smiling at me. 'She's Sister Claire of the Little Sisters of Innocence, at least she was. She isn't a nun any longer.'

'I'm not surprised,' I said acidly. 'I believe the Catholic Church to be broad-minded, but I feel that even they would draw the line at a nun in nineteen-twenties clothes visiting gambling hells with a handsome young gigolo.'

Melanie giggled.

'He's not a gigolo, he's Michel, a very nice boy,' she said, adding irrelevantly, 'He's an orphan, from the orphanage at San Sebastian.'

'I don't care if he's got six fathers,' I said – 'I want to know why this pseudo-nun is gallivanting around in Miss Booth-Wycherly's clothes.'

'Wait,' said Jean, laying a hand on my arm. 'All will be explained to you, but first come and watch her play.'

We made our way to the baccarat table and took up a station opposite to Sister Claire (who looked, I must confess, ravishing in the red velvet and yellow ostrich plumes). There was a great mound of chips in front of her, and I watched her closely as she played. She had one of those brilliant pink and white complexions like a russet autumn apple and a beautiful skin. Her cheekbones were rather high and so her blue eyes, which were enormous, looked slightly tilted and oriental. She had a well-shaped straight nose and a full, rather sensuous mouth, and her teeth when she smiled, which she often did, were small and perfect. When she smiled, her face lit up in the most extraordinary way with a sort of incandescent inner glow, and her eyes seemed to become luminous so that you felt you could almost warm your hands at them. They had the innocence and candour of a child's eyes and when she placed her bet she watched the revolutions of the wheel with the wide-eyed eager intentness of a child peering into a Christmas shop window.

The boy, whom I judged to be in his mid-twenties, was dark with a mop of curly hair, large gentle brown eyes and was handsome in a vaguely Italian gypsy sort of way. He was slender and moved with the easy grace of a dancer. There were many women in the room, both old and young, who regarded him with extreme predatory interest, but he had eyes only for Sister Claire, sitting in front of him in red velvet, turning her head to smile up at him so that the yellow ostrich feathers in her hat brushed against the front of his well-cut suit. I watched his expression as he spoke to her and mentally I apologized for calling him a gigolo. Here was a sensitive young man who was very deeply in love. That Sister Claire was in love with him was obvious, but whether she, in her innocence, recognized this I was inclined to doubt. But they seemed charmingly relaxed and happy with each other's company and they acted as if the big room was empty and they were the only two in it. They ignored the crowd which stood around watching them.

Apart from the boy, the only thing that held her full attention was the spinning wheel and the clicking ball. Having placed her bet, she would then watch the wheel with what can only be described as serenity. It was as though she was confident that the outcome would be to her advantage. Her run of luck was incredible. She obviously had no system and simply placed her chips where the spirit moved her and she was betting 50 to 100 a time. Nearly everyone at the table followed her lead. Out of twelve bets she won eleven and the croupier, with the long-suffering air of one to whom this happened all too often, pushed over some two thousand pounds' worth of chips as I watched.

'This is her last bet,' Jean said to me, in a low voice.

'How do you know?' I asked, fascinated.

'The Casino has had to come to an arrangement with her, her luck is uncanny. She only loses twice in an evening. "God's warning" she calls it, but if she played indefinitely she could cripple the Casino. The first night she played, she broke the bank. It created a sensation, I can tell you, especially when they found out who she was,' said Jean.

'But dear God, you must be joking,' I said weakly. 'I don't believe all this.'

'No, it's true,' said Jean. 'Every night her luck is the same. If she had been an ordinary person the Casino would have banned her, but when they found out she was a nun, and the centre of a cause célèbre, what could they do? Public opinion would not let them ban her. So they've had to come to an arrangement with her. She gambles once a week for three hours and when she's won two thousand five hundred pounds she stops. Of course it's worth it for the Casino, since everyone comes to see the gambling nun.'

'How did it start?' I asked, bewildered. 'And what's it got to do with Miss Booth-Wycherly's clothes, for heaven's sake?'

'Sister Claire will tell you herself,' said Jean. 'They're joining us later for supper, so possess your soul in patience until then. But you must not laugh, Gerry, for she is very serious about the whole thing.'

'Laugh?' I said. 'I'm too bewildered to laugh.'

When we got back to the flat and Jean had poured drinks for

us, we went out on to the wide veranda, cloaked with purple and salmon pink bougainvillaea, where below us the lights of Monte Carlo glittered like a carelessly emptied jewel box.

'I do feel,' I said judiciously, 'that there are certain points of this story missing. I would like to have a little background, if I may, before the nun who broke the bank at Monte Carlo arrives.'

'Well, it's only background,' said Jean. 'Sister Claire will tell you the really extraordinary part of the story'.

'Fire away,' I said.

'She was born in Devonshire, and her family were Catholic. When she was in her teens her father got a job as a gardener to a large Roman Catholic convent near Wolverhampton. She worked with him and soon she became adept at producing fruit, vegetables and flowers for the convent. The convent was a teaching one but also an orphanage and this suited Sister Claire very well for she is passionately attached to children. In her spare time she used to help the nuns with their work. When her father died she took over his job. It was then she decided to become a nun. Well, one day she saw an article about San Sebastian and the work being done by the Little Sisters of Innocence and this fired her imagination. She felt that this was a sign from God. She had always been convinced He had work for her to do and she had eagerly awaited a sign. This article was, for her, that sign. She must work at San Sebastian.'

'Wait a moment,' I protested, 'She must have read hundreds of articles in magazines. Why didn't she take those as signs?'

Jean carefully eased half an inch of white ash off the end of his cigar.

'Because,' he said, 'when you are kneeling in a flowerbed, praying for guidance, and the first thing you see when you finish is a single page from a magazine containing the article wrapped round some newly arrived seedlings, you are apt to take it as a sign, especially if you are Sister Claire.'

'I see,' I said.

'Sister Claire,' continued Jean, 'sees sermons in stones and portents in flowers and trees. Her God is everywhere, constantly

giving signs of His wishes, constantly guiding, so one must therefore be constantly on the alert to interpret His wishes. Do you
see?'

'Yes, I think I'm beginning to,' I said thoughtfully.

'Unless you can understand her deep conviction that she is
always in touch with the Almighty, you cannot understand what
made her do what she did. Also you must understand her complete
innocence. What she is convinced she was instructed to do by God
cannot possibly be wrong, and rather than not do it she would
cheerfully go to the stake. She is the stuff martyrs are made of. She
has saint's blood in her.'

He paused and refilled our glasses.

'Well, having made up her mind (and once the mind of someone
like Sister Claire is made up nothing on earth can shift it), she
moved heaven and earth until, eventually, she arrived up at San
Sebastian six years ago. She worked part time with the younger
children and ran the garden and the tiny farm with great efficiency.
And then three things happened simultaneously. First, the convent
was told it was overcrowded and would have to send half the
children elsewhere. Secondly, Michel lost his job in Monte Carlo
and retuned to the convent; thirdly, Miss Booth-Wycherly died and
left the orphanage – amongst other things – her clothes. Separately,
these things do not appear to have anything in common but put
these together and if you are Sister Claire you take it as a direct
message from heaven.'

'But I still don't see . . .' I began, when we heard the sound of
the doorbell. The maid ushered Sister Claire and Michel out on to
the veranda and, in the light of the candles set on the dining table
in the corner, the red velvet hat and dress glowed like garnets. Jean
introduced me.

'I'm delighted to meet any friend of Miss Booth-Wycherly,'
Sister Claire said, clasping my hand in both of hers, and blinding
me with the intenseness of her blue gaze. Her hands I noticed were
still rough and calloused from hard work but they were warm and
seemed to vibrate with energy as a bird vibrates when you hold it
in your cupped hands.

'You must have been shocked to learn of her death, you poor man,' she went on, 'but it is nice to know that she was an instrument of God and that she's left so much good behind her, isn't it?'

'Well,' I said, 'Jean was only just beginning to explain things to me. Perhaps you could tell me exactly what happened with this . . . er . . .'

'This miracle?' asked Sister Claire. 'Of course I will! She accepted a glass of lemonade, sipped it and then leaned forward eagerly.

'I hope I'm not a vain person, Mr Durrell,' she began, 'but ever since I was quite a young woman I have had this inner conviction that God had marked me out for some special task. I am, I regret to say, a very impatient person, it's one of my many faults and I like . . . what is the saying? Yes, I like things done yesterday, not tomorrow. But God has all the time in the world and you cannot hurry Him. Also, if He's to use you He must train you and this takes time. Then, when He is ready and He thinks you are, He gives you the signals. Do you see?'

'Yes,' I said, gravely.

'Sometimes they are very obvious signals, but sometimes they are rather obscure, I regret to say, and I fear that some one misses altogether. Monsieur Schultz told you about the magazine article?'

I nodded.

'*Such* a clear sign,' said Sister Claire, beaming at me delightedly. 'I could almost hear His voice.'

'May I suggest we move to the table and eat before supper gets cold,' said Melanie. 'You can finish your story there.'

'Of course! Of course!' cried Sister Claire. 'I'm as hungry as an orphanage full of children.'

She gave a ripple of delicious musical laughter and her eyes shone with humour. It was easy to see why Michel was in love with her. As we went to the table I walked by his side.

'Do you speak English?' I asked.

He gave me a quick smile.

'No . . . little only. Claire she teach me. She is very good for teaching,' he said proudly.

'Yes, I'm sure,' I replied.

We sat down at the table and Melanie had placed me opposite Sister Claire.

'Do please go on with your story,' said Melanie. 'I'm sure Mr Durrell won't eat a thing until he's heard it.'

'Yes, she's quite right, Sister,' I agreed.

'You must not call me Sister,' she said, and a shadow seemed to pass over her face momentarily. 'I am no longer a nun, you know.'

'I'm sorry,' I apologized. 'May I call you Miss Claire then?'

'Of course,' she said, smiling delightedly. 'I'd like that.'

She dipped her spoon into the succulent melon and sighed.

'How the children would enjoy this. I must send them some.'

'Do you still keep in er. . . . . er. . . . touch with the orphanage?' I asked, hoping to steer her back to her story.

'Keep in touch? She almost *keeps* it!' said Jean, with an explosive chuckle. Sister Claire blushed.

'I only help,' she said firmly. 'But it is only accomplished because it is God's wish that I should do so.'

There was a little silence in which I tried to imagine the Almighty instructing a nun to gamble.

'So you left Wolverhampton and came to San Sebastian,' I said at last.

She nodded.

'Yes, six years ago. As I'd had some experience in the gardens they put me in charge of their little farm. It was difficult at first as I knew nothing about cows or pigs, not even about chickens really, but I soon learnt. In my spare time I used to take the children for walks, or organize games for them – that was the part I liked best really. The children were so sweet you have no idea, then I used to grow all sorts of special things for them, like sweet corn and strawberries, which they simply loved. I was very happy, but you know even so I still felt I was not fulfilling whatever task God had ordained for me.'

She finished her melon and sat back, staring at her plate thoughtfully. Then she looked up and her blue eyes shone like sunlit sapphires.

'Then one day God began to unfold His whole plan for me. I remember I had risen early, there were several tasks I wanted to do before Mass. Well, I accomplished these so well that I had some time to spare, so after breakfast I decided to weed the flowerbed outside Sister Mary's windows. I had laid out a small flowerbed there because Sister Mary did so enjoy flowers, but I'd been so busy with the farm that I'm afraid I had neglected it. Dandelions are excellent in the salad but they are not excellent in herbaceous borders. It was a warm day I remember and the windows of Sister Mary's office were open, so I could hear every word that was said inside. I do assure you that I was not eavesdropping. In fact, when I first heard the voices, I was about to make my presence known and to leave but it was the first sentence that made my blood run cold, and I assure you I just sat there as though I was in a trance. I know now of course that God intended me to hear, but I did not realize it then. It was the Mayor of San Sebastian who was talking to Sister Mary and what he said was, "So, Sister, I'm afraid if you cannot build a new wing on the orphanage you will have to send some of the children away."

'You may imagine my horror at hearing this. To part with some of the children, most of whom had been with us for several years, and who looked upon the orphanage as home and us as their parents, was unthinkable. Sister Mary, of course, said it was impossible to build a new wing as we had only just enough money to keep going. The Mayor, who was a good, kind man, said he fully realized this and he knew the children weren't suffering, even if they did have to sleep six to a room. But the council had decreed that it was unhygienic and unsuitable and this was their decision. Then he left, telling Sister Mary that she had three weeks to give him a reply before the next council meeting. I can't tell you the black despair that seized me. I knew that Sister Mary could do nothing and that we would have to lose some of our children. I am afraid I was weak enough to give way to despair and I cried. When I had recovered myself, I realized God would not let this happen, and so I prayed to him for guidance. It was then that the first miracle occurred.'

The maid placed a bowl of crimson wild strawberries in front of Sister Claire and flanked it with a jug of cream.

'Oh, fraises du bois,' cried Sister Claire delightedly. 'I used to take the children out into the woods at San Sebastian and we used to collect them and take them back to the orphanage. I fear they used to eat more than they took back, but they did enjoy it.'

'What was the first miracle?' I asked, determined that Sister Claire should not be side-tracked.

'Oh, yes, well that of course was Michel losing his job. Michel was one of our children, but long before my time. Sister Mary had got him a job in a bakery in Monte Carlo, but the old man, the baker, fell sick and had to close down. So Michel came back to the orphanage and he arrived the very day that Sister Mary had the bad news. She called me into her office and I thought she was going to tell me about the Mayor's visit. I was going to confess that I had heard it all. But she didn't say a word about it and I realized that she was not going to burden the rest of us with this worry, but she was going to try and solve the problem herself. No, what she wanted to see me about was Michel. She said that while she was trying to find him another job she thought he could work with me on the farm, for she knew there were several things that needed doing that were beyond my strength. I was delighted, for it meant that I could get the cowshed roof repaired and . . . oh well . . . a host of other things . . . and Michel was so strong and good with his hands. So he came to work with me and we managed to get so much done together. Well, one day I told him I had always felt that God had work for me to do and that he would give me a sign. To anyone else I expect I would have sounded presumptuous but Michel understood completely. Indeed, he was so sympathetic that I felt impelled to tell him about the awful thing that had happened to the orphanage because it was preying on my mind. He was as shocked and horrified as I was, but we talked about it and neither of us could see any way of solving the problem.

'Then the second miracle happened. Sister Mary called me to her office and told me that poor Miss Booth-Wycherly had died and left all her clothes and furniture to us. She asked me to take Michel down to Monte Carlo and pack up Miss Booth-Wycherly's clothes and arrange to have them brought up to the orphanage and then to have the furniture sold. Now, I had never been to Monte Carlo before, but of course Michel had and knew his way about. We took the bus down and really I can remember it being quite a shock, quite bewildering you know. It was so long since I had been in a city, it took my breath away. I felt stunned by all the noise and activity. The whole time I was there I was in a sort of daze.'

Sister Claire paused and took a sip of lemonade.

'I'm afraid I'm talking an awful lot,' she said apologetically. 'I do hope I'm not boring you.'

A chorus of voices assured her that she was not boring us.

'Well,' she went on, 'when we got to Miss Booth-Wycherly's home I must admit I was a little surprised and disappointed, for Michel had been so sure that we would find something of value that would help save the orphanage. I could see that the furniture was so worm-eaten that it would not fetch a good price, and the clothes, though beautifully kept, I felt were too old-fashioned to sell. But there were piles and piles of them. Such beautiful materials. I'd never seen so many clothes for one person.'

'I know,' I said. 'She once gave me a fashion show of her clothes and it lasted three hours. It ended with the gown she had worn for the dance that King Edward VII had attended, a blue and white silk gown and a blue and gold velvet cloak. It was a startlingly beautiful get-up and I thought she must have looked ravishing in it when she was young. No wonder Edward pinched her bottom.'

'Gerry!' said Melanie, but Sister Claire only chuckled.

'I'm glad you saw the cloak and remember it,' she said. 'It was that cloak that really started the whole thing.'

'How?' I said, astonished, remembering Miss Booth-Wycherly pirouetting in front of me, making the heavy blue velvet cloak lined with gold brocade shimmer and curl in blue waves around her.

'Well, naturally, we had to unpack all the clothes and examine them,' she went on. 'They were all beautifully kept in tissue paper and camphor, but even so I felt we had to make sure they were all right. It was quite a job, I can tell you, unpacking and then repacking all those clothes, and at the same time, it was really rather exciting, like unpacking a rainbow. Then at the very bottom of one of the trunks we found a very large cardboard box, and inside it were the dress and cloak you described. Now, the box was a big one and filled the whole of the bottom of the trunk. Michel was doing the unpacking and took the lid off the box and lifted out the gown. Do you remember how it was embroidered around the neck and sleeves with small white beads like pearls? Michel held up the dress and said how he wished they were real pearls, so that we could sell them and the orphanage would never have to worry again. I said that I felt sure that if God wished us to have the money for the orphanage He would show us the way, and as I was saying it, Michel pulled the cloak out of the box. Remember the blue and gold cloak, so beautiful, like summer skies and buttercups? A corner of it caught on the edge of the box and lifted it up, and underneath where it must have slipped ages and ages ago was a small bag. It was a tiny thing made out of the same materials as the cloak and with a golden clasp and a short golden chain handle. My first thought was of Lina – she was a young girl at the orphanage and she loved pretty things – for I felt that this bag would be a wonderful gift for her, and then of course I realized that the other children would be jealous. You know they can't help it sometimes, poor little things. Anyway, I picked up the bag and at once I noticed something curious about it.'

She paused and sipped her lemonade. To say you could have heard a pin drop would have been an understatement. Jean eased the ash off the end of his cigar as if he feared the sound of it landing in the ash-tray might start an avalanche.

'The thing I noticed was that it was extraordinarily heavy for such a small bag,' continued Sister Claire. 'It puzzled me, for the chain and the catch were obviously not gold, so it was not those that made it heavy. It was something inside. So I opened it and I could hardly believe my eyes. It was the third miracle. Do you know what was inside, Mr Durrell? Twenty-one sovereigns. They were fat and golden and sort of rich-looking. I don't know how to describe it – when they moved together they didn't chink like ordinary money, they made quite a different sound, you know, like the difference between pouring milk and cream. Do you think that's silly?'

'I know exactly what you mean,' I said.

'Well, of course, Michel went absolutely mad when he saw the money, silly boy,' she said, smiling affectionately at him. 'He danced round the room, shouting that God had answered our prayers and the orphanage was saved. It took me some moments to quieten him. Mind you, I was a bit dazed myself, but I did realize that it would take more than twenty-one sovereigns to solve the orphanage's problems. Well, we sat down and discussed it. Michel insisted that he ought to take the sovereigns to the bank to find out what they were worth, so we went to the Credit Lyonnais, a great big place, do you know it? On Boulevard Saint-Martin. It looked more like a palace or a great hotel than a bank, with a marble floor and everything. I was almost afraid to go in, but Michel forced me to. He has such self-confidence. Well, when the clerk saw what we had, he gave us a very peculiar look. I was embarrassed and felt sure he thought we had come by them dishonestly. He said we had better see the manager. So, after a moment we were taken into the manager's office. Such a sumptuous office it was, with great leather chairs and a simply huge desk like a dining table. Monsieur Fulvard – that was the manager's name – was such a kind, helpful man. He first asked us how we had come by our treasure and so I had to tell him all about Miss Booth-Wycherly's clothes and how we had found the sovereigns and he was most impressed and agreed that it was indeed a miracle. Then he called in a charming young man who was . . . well . . . I suppose he was a sort of gold expert. He took the coins away to measure them or weigh them or whatever it is they do with them.

'When he had gone, Monsieur Fulvard explained to us that the miracle was really a double one. You see, the coins were valuable because they were made of gold, but also because they were of a certain year – 1875 – this made them much more valuable. Apparently, there are people who collect coins, I didn't know this but it is quite true. Such a curious thing to collect, isn't it? Monsieur said that he had a friend who was a coin collector, and a very honest man, and if we would allow him, he would telephone his friend and ask him to make us an offer. Of course, I felt that this side of things should be left to Sister Mary, but Michel pointed out that she would have to do all this anyway, so we were simply saving her trouble.

'Monsieur Fulvard's friend came round straight away. He seemed absolutely delighted with the coins and then, I must say to my amazement, he offered us what I thought was an enormous sum. He said that if they'd been just ordinary coins – that sounds silly, but you know what I mean – they would have been worth a hundred thousand francs but as they'd been minted, I think that's the right word, in 1875 they were worth double that. As you may imagine, both Michel and I simply could not believe our ears, nor our eyes as Monsieur Fulvard counted out the notes. It seemed, at first, a gigantic fortune, something we couldn't even imagine. I kept thinking how delighted Sister Mary would be when we showed her the money, such beautifully coloured notes, you have no idea. I know it seems silly, but they reminded me of Miss Booth-Wycherly's clothes. They rustled like her clothes did when we unpacked them. I have never held so much money in my life.'

She paused and took some more lemonade. My coffee sat cold and untouched in front of me, so fascinated was I by her story.

'What did you put the notes in?' I asked, for I knew that most nuns' robes had capacious pockets, not unlike poachers' pockets, built into them.

'I put them in Miss Booth-Wycherly's bag,' she said. 'Where else? That, after all, is where we found the coins. I felt she would have liked it.'

'Indeed she would,' I said, warmly, imagining Miss Booth-Wycherly's delight if she could have witnessed the scene.

'So we went back to the flat,' said Sister Claire, 'and I don't mind admitting we found some coffee in the kitchen and we made ourselves a cup to revive ourselves. It was while we were having coffee that we really sat down and tried to work out what the money could do for the orphanage. Do you know, it came as an awful shock, I mean to have that great mass of notes, but to realize that it just might build an extra room. I can't tell you how downcast we were. For both of us stupidly had visions of being able to build another twenty or thirty bedrooms, showers and everything. It was a bitter disappointment. It was then, of course, while we were so depressed, that Michel had his idea.

'As we were leaving Monsieur Fulvard's office, the bank manager had cautioned me not to spend all the money at the Casino, just as a joke, of course. Well, I'd heard of the Casino, naturally, but I didn't really realize what it was then. Well, while we were sitting drinking our coffee, Michel reminded me of what Monsieur Fulvard had said, and he suggested that the way to make the money grow was in fact through the Casino. Of course, I was adamant that this was impossible. I said so, quite firmly. But I must say somewhat to my surprise Michel was equally firm. He asked me whether or not I thought God was guiding me. Of course, I had to say yes. Then he listed all the things that had happened recently – his arrival, poor Miss Booth-Wycherly's death, her legacy and the finding of the coins, and then finding they were worth double . . . he asked me if I believed that this was God's design. Of course, I had to admit that I felt it was, because deep inside myself this is what I did feel. I felt somehow, though I was not sure how, that God was moving me towards the work that he was intending me to do. Michel said that he felt that, too, and this made him an instrument of God just as much as I was. He said that the only way we could make the money grow was by going to the Casino. He said that after all we were only doing what Jesus had done with the loaves and the fishes, though of course not in quite the same way. I must say he was very forceful and convincing and I felt myself, in spite of my better judgement, beginning to waver. He then said that he wouldn't even risk Miss Booth-Wycherly's money. He still had a small amount of his wages from his job, and he would wager these first. If God wanted us to increase the legacy this way, we would surely win. We had another cup of coffee and argued about it, I'm afraid, for I was not altogether convinced. But you should have seen Michel! He was so persuasive, so loquacious, his eyes positively shone! In the end, I had to admit that it did seem that it was God's plan that, having got that amount of money, we should increase it.

'Michel said that I should stay in the flat while he went to the Casino and then if he was successful he would come back to me for the money. But there were two things against this. First, I did not want him going to the Casino alone. I knew that in some ways he is more worldly than I am, but I still felt that he was very young to do this on his own. The second point was his clothing. He was wearing only some very old and patched jeans and a threadbare shirt. I felt sure that if he turned up looking so young and such a . . . such a *ragamuffin*, they wouldn't let him in. Then Michel had an idea. He suggested that we both dressed up in Miss Booth-Wycherly's clothes and went to the Casino.'

I gazed at Sister Claire, unable to comment, for the idea of a nun in Miss Booth-Wycherly's clothes was in itself unbelievable, let alone a nun gambling in them. But as well as this, for her to be accompanied by a boy in drag lifted the whole thing into the realms of fantasy. I found myself smiling in spite of my effort to wear a grave and attentive expression. Sister Claire blushed.

'Of course, I was adamant,' she said, just a shade defensively. 'I said that such idea was quite impossible. But Michel stood firm. He said that God had shown us the way and for us to lose courage now would mean that we had no faith in His design. He said that, in his opinion, God had given us proof after proof of what we should do, and he felt that it would be cowardly of us to give up now, when we were in sight of success. I remained unconvinced, though I had to admit that all the signs appeared to indicate that God wanted us to increase His bounty – but doing it at the Casino, that was the thing that worried me. In any case, I pointed out, Miss Booth-Wycherly's clothes probably wouldn't fit us. So then Michel said that, if the clothes fitted us, would I take it as a sign that God wanted us to go to the Casino? Well, of course, I thought it was too ridiculous. I mean, Michel and I are the same height and build, but the clothes looked huge, somehow. So, naturally, jokingly, I said that if the clothes fitted I would go, never dreaming for a moment that there was any possibility.'

She paused and laced her fingers together, placing them on the table-cloth.

'Well, of course they fitted perfectly, as you can see.' She held out her arm and the crimson velvet caught the light, red as blood and dark as wine in the folds.

'As a matter of fact,' she confessed, 'Michel made a very good girl, really very pretty, if you can use that word to describe a boy. He chose a simple yellow silk dress, with shoes to match and a black and yellow hat, rather tight-fitting – I think they call them cloche hats, and his hair being curly and fairly long, it made him look as though he had one of those short haircuts that so many girls seem to be wearing nowadays. He insisted that I wore the blue and white dress and the cloak, because he said that these were the clothes that had helped us find the money.'

She paused and gave a tiny cough and smiled apologetically.

'I'm afraid I'm talking too much,' she said. 'I'm giving myself a sore throat. I wonder, if it's no trouble, may I have a Perrier water?'

Perrier was produced at once. Sister Claire drank half a glass as if it were a rare vintage, cleared her throat and smiled round at us ravishingly.

'You have absolutely no idea how very curious ordinary clothes felt after a habit,' she confessed. 'I really felt like . . . well, I don't know what . . . yes I do . . . it was when I was young and at Christmas we used to play charades – you know, you dressed up in curious clothes and somehow you didn't really feel like you, if you know what I mean? That was exactly how I felt. As a matter of fact, I felt really shy – just as I did, you know, when we used to play charades, and awkward, you know. I kept feeling I might trip over the dress, and then of course Michel looked so funny as a girl, and this made me . . . I mean he looked so like a girl . . . it made me laugh, and then this of course made him laugh. So really we laughed so much it was quite some time before we were fit to go to the Casino.'

She stopped and slowly savoured the remains of her Perrier.

'I'm afraid I'm describing it very badly,' she apologized, 'but it's difficult to explain exactly how all the events of that day built up. Looking back on it, I'm astonished that I did what I did, but I suppose everyone who is guided by God feels the same. But it was when we actually got to the Casino that I really faltered. It was so huge, rather as I imagined St Peter's in Rome to be, though of course not built for the same purpose. All those columns as we went in, all the marble. I didn't know there was so much marble in the world. I was very afraid that they would see that Michel was not a girl, and I couldn't help feeling that somehow they would guess that I was a nun, though goodness knows how, seeing the clothes I was wearing. He went in, and I had to rely entirely on Michel of course, and he had never been to the Casino himself, but the baker he worked for had frequently gone, and he had told Michel all about it. Michel decided that we should try the chemin de fer, and so we approached the table. Everyone looked at us curiously, but I know now that it was because of the clothes. I know people wear eccentric clothes nowadays, but you must admit that Miss Booth-Wycherly's clothes were a little extraordinary, even by today's standards. Of course, I didn't know what to do, but Michel soon showed me. He was so clever, considering he had never gambled before. For our first bet we used only the minimum stake. I'd said to Michel that if we didn't win with the first bet this was a sign that God did not want us to gamble. We placed it on the red and I must admit my heart was in my mouth as the ball whirled round and round.'

She took a sip of Perrier and gazed at us with a sort of serene triumph.

'Of course, we won,' she said. 'It was for me a clear sign. I now knew at last what it was that God intended I should do. It was like a glow inside me, you know, I simply knew for certain that my hand was being guided, that I was merely the instrument. I was so sure that before Michel could stop me I placed all our money on the next bet. He was horrified, but I told him that he must trust in God. Of course we won again and twenty-four times after that. Twice we lost, but on each occasion I'd only felt that I should put on a small bet and so the loss was not great. After three hours' play, we had made over two million francs. Michel wanted me to go on, but I felt it was time to stop, and to go back and tell Sister Mary the good news.

'So we returned to San Sebastian, after changing our clothes, of course, and we were so excited, you have no idea. You see, not only had we started to really help the orphanage but I felt that I had at last been shown my true vocation.'

She paused and gave a tiny sob.

'Unfortunately, the Reverend Mother didn't see it this way. I was most distressed, for she was considerably shocked. She felt that not only had I done something terrible because I was a nun, but that I had led Michel into temptation. She did not seem to realize that it was God's plan and nothing I could say would alter her opinion. So I was expelled from the Order.'

'You weren't!' I said, incredulous.

'Yes, Gerry, it was such a cruel thing to do,' said Jean, heavily.

'However,' said Sister Claire, wiping her eyes, 'Michel was staunchly with me. I still do not think we are wrong. A gift given by God cannot be bad, especially if it is used for good purposes. I believe that God gave me the ability to . . . to . . . to gamble in order to help the children. I was determined not to go against His wishes . . . it seemed to me it would be a sin. So, through a second-hand dealer, I bought Miss Booth-Wycherly's clothes from the convent – because it was obvious that it was her clothes that the Almighty wanted me to wear – and I went on gambling. When I had raised a significant sum of money, I sent a cheque to the Mother Superior, saying it was money from God. She sent the cheque back saying that, in the eyes of the Almighty, it would be like accepting money from prostitution. For days I was so distraught that poor Michel was at his wits' end. You understand, here I had an enormous sum of money which God had shown me how to earn and what purpose to put it to, and now I was being defeated. It was then that Michel had his brilliant idea. Mother Superior, of course, knew my name and where I had the bank account, so any money coming from that source would be refused by her. So, we decided to open a new bank account in Michel's name, so the money would be accepted. Of course, he had no name, poor dear, because . . . because . . . well, because. So we had to find a new one.'

She leaned forward, her eyes blazing.

'It's such *fun* to be able to choose your own name. All of us have our names wished on us by our parents. But to be able to choose – why, it's like being born again.'

'So what name did he choose?' I asked.

Sister Claire looked at me in wide-eyed astonishment. 'Why, Booth-Wycherly, of course,' she said.

I stared at her lovely face for a moment and then I started to laugh. Jean and Melanie joined me, for the jest was rich. Soon, incited by our laughter, but not completely understanding it, Sister Claire and Michel joined us.

As we laughed, I am sure that somewhere in that terra incognita we call Heaven, Miss Booth-Wycherly was laughing too.

A Parrot for the Parson

She came flying down the platform wearing an elegant blue tweed suit and a blue tam-o'shanter that made her ultra-marine eyes look twice their size.

'Darling, I'm here. It's *me*, Ursula,' she cried out, as she dodged like a rugger player round people, baggage and porters. She flung herself into my arms, fastened her lovely mouth on mine and indulged in the loud buzzing noise she made whenever her lips made contact with mine. All the men on the platform stared at me with envy and all the women stared at Ursula with hatred as she was so radiant and lovely.

'Darling,' she said at last, removing her mouth, 'I missed you most *dreadfully*.'

'But I only saw you the day before yesterday,' I protested, trying to disentangle myself from her vice-like grip.

'Yes, but darling, it was such a *long* yesterday,' she said and kissed me once more. 'Oh darling, to be with you in London in the spring. How scrumptious,' she said.

'Where's your luggage?' I asked.

'The porter's bringing it,' she said, pointing down the platform to where an extremely elderly porter was struggling with four large suitcases and a hatbox and a huge brass cage containing a grey parrot.

'What the hell have you brought a parrot for?' I asked, filled with alarm.

'Darling, his name is Moses and he talks beautifully, even though he does use a lot of bad language. I bought him off a sailor, so I suppose the sailor taught him. You know how uncouth sailors are, when they're not being captains or admirals. I'm sure Nelson never swore. I mean, he might have said the odd damn when he lost his arm and his eye, but I think that was permissible, don't you?'

As usual, when coming in contact with my favourite girlfriend, I began to feel a sense of unreality creeping over me.

'But what do you want a parrot for? You can't keep him at the hotel.'

'Don't be silly, darling, Claridge's keep anything for you. He's a present for the Reverend Penge, who's very sick, poor dear.'

My mind reeled. This was obviously yet another of Ursula's charitable deeds which always caused disaster, and I was caught up in the middle of it. Leaving the subject of the parrot for a moment I looked at her mountain of suitcases and the hatbox.

'Do you really need all that luggage?' I enquired. 'Or are you planning to stay in London permanently?'

'Don't be silly, darling, that's only for three days and I knew you wanted me to look nice,' she said. 'Why, I've scarcely brought *anything*, only the bare essentials. After all, you don't want me to go about nude, do you?'

'I refuse to reply to that question for fear of being incriminated,' I said.

We arrived at the taxi rank, the luggage was stowed and Moses in his cage was installed in the back. As he was doing this, the porter was unwise enough to say 'Pretty Polly' to Moses, who, with a clarity of diction I have rarely heard equalled in a parrot, told the porter where he should go and what he should do to himself when he got there, both suggestions geographically and biologically impossible.

'Do you think this parrot is a wise gift to give a reverend gentleman in frail health?' I asked my beautiful companion as the taxi started in the direction of Claridge's.

Ursula turned her magnetic blue eyes on me in puzzlement. 'But of course,' she said, 'because it talks.'

'Well, I know it talks,' I said. 'It's what it says that worries me.' As if on cue, Moses opened his beak and spoke again.

'Oooh Charlie boy, oh let's do it again, Charlie boy. Oh I do love a cuddle. Heh, heh, heh, there's nothing like a cuddle.'

'You see what I mean,' I said. 'Do you think your kind gesture is wise?'

'Well, I'll have to tell you about poor old Reverend Penge,' said Ursula. 'He was the vicar of Portel-cum-Hardy, a tiny village near where we live and he got himself into terrible trouble with the choir.'

'You mean a mixed choir, or just boys?' I asked.

'No, no, they were just boys,' she said. 'Well, I mean nobody would have worried if it had been just one teeny-weeny choirboy, but naturally when it came to a whole choir the villagers got up in arms. As they said – and I think quite rightly – there is a limit. Enough's enough.'

'How big was the choir?'

'Oh, I think about ten but I'm not sure,' she said. 'But I thought the vicar was a very nice man and they should not have black-balled him from the Church.'

'Is that what they did?' I asked, fascinated.

'Yes,' she said, a trifle uncertainly, 'or maybe because the Church is so pure they whiteballed him. I'm not sure. Anyway, poor dear, he's living in one room somewhere off the King's Road and he wrote me the most pathetic letter saying how ill he was and how he had no one to talk to, so that is why I bought him a parrot.'

'But of course,' I said, resignedly. 'What better present for a whiteballed vicar than a foul-mouthed parrot.'

'It was the only thing,' said Ursula. 'After all, I couldn't very well bring him a choirboy, now could I? Do be sensible, darling.'

I sighed.

'Why are you staying at Claridge's and not at my hotel?' I asked.

'I don't like the hotel you stay in, darling. One of the waiters smells of cod-liver oil and besides Daddy always stays at Claridge's – it's like the pub round the corner,' she said.

Moses ruffled his feathers and vouchsafed something to us.

'Get your pants down, get your pants down, let's have a peek,' he said.

'Don't you think that perhaps a small, inarticulate choirboy would have been preferable?' I asked.

'Don't be silly, darling. Anyway, he could go to prison if it was inarticulate.'

'If who was inarticulate?' I asked, bewildered.

'The choirboy. It's called reducing a miner,' she said. 'Although I've never understood what a miner's got to do with choirboys since choirboys are choirboys and miners work digging coal.'

As usual in a conversation with Ursula, I was left in a state of such puzzlement that it was best to drop the whole subject and start again.

'When are we going to get rid of Moses?' I asked.

'Moses knows,' said Moses. 'Moses knows – heh, heh, heh – drop your pants, there's a good boy.'

'Tomorrow morning. I thought we'd take him first thing,' she said.

'Moses likes a bit of bum,' said Moses.

'I still think that with this parrot's preoccupation with sex it is an unwise gift,' I said. 'You might have the Reverend Penge scooting down to St Paul's Cathedral in search of more choirboys, incited by Moses's licentiousness.'

'Go stuff yourself,' said Moses, fixing me with a glittering eye.

'Darling, the Reverend Penge can't go scooting anywhere; Ursula explained patiently, 'he's old and very fragile. He can't go pursuing choirboys. He can't run as fast as they can. They would have to be brought to him. I mean, of course, one wouldn't want that, but you know what I mean.'

'Yes,' I said. 'I'm only surprised you didn't get him a sheepdog.'

'A sheepdog!' she said in amazement. 'Whatever for?'

'For rounding up the choirboys,' I explained.

Ursula looked at me severely.

'You know, darling, there are times when you don't seem to take life seriously enough.'

I gazed at her four suitcases, her hatbox and at Moses in his cage and then gazed deeply into her lovely eyes.

'I'm sorry,' I said contritely. 'I'll try being less frivolous in future.'

'That's right, darling,' she said. 'If you try, you can take life as seriously as I do.'

'I will do my very best,' I said.

She linked her arm through mine and gave me a brief kiss.

'Darling, isn't it going to be divine,' she said dreamily. 'Three days in London with you – how truly scrumptious.'

'Moses likes a bit of bum,' said Moses.

'Darling, I do see what you mean,' said Ursula thoughtfully. 'He does seem terribly preoccupied with bits of the body.'

'Don't worry,' I said, 'I expect the Reverend Penge was too. I'm sure they will get on splendidly.'

'You know, you are a comfort to me,' she said, snuggling up and gazing at me with her huge eyes. 'Whenever I'm in doubt about something, I say to myself, "What would Gerry have done?"'

'And then you do the opposite,' I said.

'No, darling, you're being modest,' she said. 'Everything I do is based on your advice.'

Seeing that Ursula left behind her, in her efforts to help people, a trail of carnage worse than a dinosaur in a china shop, this was scant praise.

'In fact,' she went on, 'there was a point when I was seriously thinking about falling in love with you, but I decided not to.'

'Good heavens!' I exclaimed. 'When did I get this reprieve?'

'Well, it was some time ago, on the beach under the pier when we were swimming and you said that I'd got a bottom like a cherry stone,' she said. 'It was very hurtful.'

'I'm sorry if I hurt your feelings, sweetheart, but you know cherubs were painted by all the best painters in all the best positions and looked delightful.'

'What sort of painters?' she asked suspiciously.

'Well, all the most famous medieval ones,' I said, wishing I had not brought up the subject.'

'You mean like Bottomcelli?' she asked.

'Yes,' I said, 'he painted the most beautiful bottoms in the business, hence his name, and he would have been captivated by yours.'

'Really, darling? How wonderful. It's nice to know there's one man in the world who appreciates your bottom,' she said. 'Come to think of it, it's not often that your bottom gets adulated. I suppose it's because it's always *under* you. It's all to do with modesty. I suppose that's why they say hiding your bum under a bushel, because if you have a behind like a Cherubum you don't want it displayed to all and sultry.'

'It's a very old English saying,' I said resignedly.

I had once thought of buying Ursula a dictionary, but discarded the idea when I found out she could not spell.

When we reached Claridge's, our taxi door was smartly opened by the immaculately top-hatted doorman who hooked a white-gloved finger into the brass loop at the top of the cage and wafted it out. It became immediately obvious that Moses had been enjoying the taxi ride and took grave exception to its being interrupted. The doorman lifted the parrot cage the better to view the bird and was just going to say smilingly, 'Pretty Polly' when Moses fixed him with a brilliant stare and said, with searing malevolence, 'You bastard son of a ditch-delivered whore!' The words were spoken with such venom and clarity that the doorman reeled back as if he had stepped on the wrong end of a rake.

Ursula was out of the taxi with the speed and agility of an eel. 'Oh, how kind of you to carry Moses,' she smiled, turning some twenty-five thousand watts of her personality on to the man. 'He's a parrot, you know, and he can talk *beautifully*. Unfortunately, he's having trouble with his eyes – it's a parrot disease called Parotitis and we've brought him up to Harley Street to have his eyes tested – you see, he's mistaking people for other people. He must have mistaken you for somebody he dislikes. He'll be right as rain when he's been fitted up with a new pair of spectacles.'

'Moses likes a pair of testicles,' Moses remarked conversationally. Faced with the whole improbable scene for which his training had not prepared him, the doorman looked stunned.

'Does madam wish to have this talking bird in her room?' he asked at last.

'Oh, yes, please,' said Ursula, 'and all this baggage. You are kind.' She turned back and leant into the taxi.

'I forgot to bring his damned cover,' she said. 'Once that's over him, he doesn't say a word. I'll have to buy another. Goodbye, darling, see you at lunch. One sharp at the Dorchester. I love you to bits.'

She kissed me and followed the parrot into Claridge's. Moses was now singing in a fine, rich, ringing baritone, 'Aint't it a pity she's only one titty to feed the baby on. Poor little bugger will never play rugger and grow up big and strong.'

I gave the driver the address of my hotel and sat back, mopping my brow.

'A right little lady you've got there, guy,' said the driver. 'She's a real card, if you don't mind me saying so.'

'She's a whole deck of cards,' I said bitterly.

The driver chuckled.

'And that there parrot,' he said. 'Laugh? I could've killed myself listening to 'im. A real pornographic parrot that one and no mistake.'

'Yes, the two of them make an enchanting couple,' I said, acidly.

'Yuss,' said the driver, 'but if I had to choose, straight up, I'd choose that parrot.'

'Why?' I asked, faintly insulted at this implied slur on Ursula's charms.

'Well, put it this way, guy,' he said, 'if the parrot got a bit much you could always strangle him. But your lady, well, she's far too beautiful to strangle, i'nt she, ay?'

'Yes,' I sighed, 'although the thought has not infrequently crossed my mind.'

He laughed as he drew up outside my hotel and swivelled round to grin at me.

'She's got you 'ooked, guv, if you don't mind my saying so. Like a stray dawg we got once. I says to the wife, I says, "We don't want no bleedin' dog, take 'im to Battersea Dogs' 'ome," I says.

But d'you know, guy, it was so damn charming we couldn't bear the thought of 'im being put down. So we've still got 'im. It's like that with women,' he said, philosophically, 'once you're 'ooked you can't bear to 'ave' em put down, in a manner of speaking. That'll be three pound eleven and six, guv, please.'

'The trouble is,' I said, as I paid him, 'there's no Battersea Dogs' Home I could send her to.'

'No, but there's always your own 'ome,' he said, chuckling. 'Good luck, guy.'

I went up to my room, laid out my best suit and a clean shirt on the bed, together with a rather startling tie brought back as an unexpected present from Lisbon by my brother-in-law, made sure my socks had no holes in them and that my shoes were polished. Taking Ursula out to a meal was always a traumatic affair, so I wanted to be sure I did not commit any social solecisms of my own. Hers were quite enough to cope with.

I got to the Dorchester on the dot of one and I was just straightening my tie and waiting for Ursula's arrival when the head waiter, whom I knew from other occasions, came hurrying towards me.

'Good morning, Sebastian,' I said, jovially.

'Good morning, sir. Madam is already at the table.'

This sounded ominous. Ursula was never on time, let alone early. Sebastian led me to a table for four, but there was no sign of Ursula.

'I think perhaps madam has gone to the powder room,' Sebastian vouchsafed. I sat down, drew up my chair and my feet were brought up short by a metallic clang. I lifted the table-cloth and from within his cage Moses regarded me with disfavour. In two pungent words he told me what to do. My blood ran cold.

Sebastian, his eyes on the ceiling, was unsuccessfully trying to conceal a smile behind a menu card.

'What the hell's this?' I asked.

'I believe it to be a bird belonging to madam,' said Sebastian suavely, 'a member of the parrot tribe, so I am told. Madam arrived with it and wished it put beneath the table. Its name, I am informed, is Moses. When it arrived in the foyer, it was quite –

er – loquacious and, considering its name, its language was not exactly biblical.'

'You don't have to tell me,' I said bitterly. 'How the hell did you get it in here without it insulting all your customers?'

'With the aid of napkins wrapped round the cage,' said Sebastian. 'Madam said that darkness had a soothing and soporific effect on the bird and deadened its loquacity and so it appears. Apart from that little exchange with you it has not proffered any remarks since we put it under the table.'

'But why in God's name did she bring it here?' I asked, exasperatedly.

'I may be wrong, but I believe madam brought it along in the nature of a surprise present for yourself, sir.'

'Surprise present?' I snorted. 'I wouldn't have this bloody bird with a crock of gold.'

'I must admit . . .' said Sebastian. 'Ah, here is madam now. She will doubtless explain the presence of – er – Moses, if I may be so bold as to address him by his first name.'

I looked at his twinkling eyes.

'Sebastian,' I said, 'madam will have a dry martini and I will have a large Scotch and Perrier. Oh, and if you have any hemlock, bring a beakerful for the parrot.'

He bowed and pulled out a chair as the reason for all my woes approached the table.

'Hello, darling,' she cried. 'Aren't you pleased I'm so early?'

'You're *both* early,' I said ominously. She gave a guilty start.

'Oh, so you've discovered Moses then?' she said attempting a lighthearted tone.

'It would be a bit difficult to miss him,' I said acidly. 'The toes of both my carefully polished shoes are being scraped to hell under his damn cage, and my left shoe is rapidly filling up with sand and what my limited horticultural knowledge tells me must be sunflower seed. Or it may of course even be manure. Why, might I ask, do we have to have Moses partaking of luncheon with us?'

'Now, darling, don't start getting angry with me. I hate it when you get angry and starting roaring and snorting like Achilles the Bun.'

'Attila,' I corrected. I was too dispirited to correct the Bun part. Ursula looked at me and her eyes welled. Two enormous tears, bright as shooting stars, raced down her cheeks.

'Darling,' she said huskily, 'I've had a horrible time, so don't be so cruel to me! I was just about to relent when she added, 'Or to poor Moses.'

At that moment the drinks arrived and this successfully prevented me from telling her what I thought of 'poor Moses'. I toasted her in a chilly silence while from those springs she possessed 'in caverns measureless to man', she allowed two more tears of improbable size to slide down her cheeks. At that moment, before my heart could melt at this display of emotion – which I knew to be entirely spurious – Sebastian appeared, bearing menus and a wine list.

'Sir, madam,' he said, slightly bowing as he handed out the menus, 'we have some rather lovely things today. The grilled lambs' kidneys are superb, the oysters Rockefeller are especially large and succulent . . .'

'Do you have any roast parrot?' I enquired. 'West African grey for preference.'

Ursula glared at me.

'You don't eat parrots,' she said.

'Yes, you do, if you're a West African,' I replied.

'To answer your question, sir,' said Sebastian smoothly, 'we have none on the menu. We have been told that they are tough and indigestible and have the unfortunate effect of making you talk in your sleep.'

Both of us laughed and peace reigned.

'So tell me why I am having lunch at the Dorchester with what my friend the taxi driver called a pornographic parrot,' I suggested.

'Well, darling, I got him into my room safely enough, although I had to give the porter an enormous tip because Moses called him – well, never mind. Anyway, I wanted to go out and do a bit of shopping, some things I forgot to bring, and get some fruit for Moses. Then I noticed his water dish was empty, poor dear, and he was obviously thirsty, so I got him a vodka and tonic from the fridge in the bedroom . . .'

'You got him a *what*?' I interrupted incredulously.

'A vodka and tonic, darling. You know, that Russian drink the Vulgar boatmen used to have. The sailor I got him from told me he never drank anything else. Well, he must have been dying of thirst, poor lamb, because he simply lapped it up. Then he went into a sort of doze.'

'I'm not surprised,' I said.

'So I gave him another one in case he should wake up and still feel thirsty . . .'

'*Another* one!' I interjected. 'Sweetheart, you must be mad.'

'But why?' asked Ursula, puzzled. 'I mean, I don't like vodka, but that's no reason why he shouldn't drink it. After all, I don't see why I should start acting like those Intemperance people telling people what to do.'

'Quite,' I said.

'It's that sort of thing that leads to crime,' she explained mysteriously, 'interfering with people's civil liberties and making them uncivil.'

'So after you got him fit to be tied, what did you do?' I enquired.

'Fit to be tied? What does that mean?' she asked.

'It's an American expression; it means now you'd got him so drunk you had to tie him up.'

'But I didn't have to tie him up,' she said triumphantly. 'He fell on the floor of the cage. It gave me quite a shock. I thought he was dead until I heard him snoring.'

'And then?' I asked, fascinated in spite of myself.

'Well, I went down to Fortnum and Mason to get his food.'

'Fortnum and Mason? Why not to some little fruiterers in the back streets round there?'

'What, and be seen walking into Claridge's with a lot of brown paper bags? Darling, do be sensible.'

'Well, you didn't seem to mind walking into Claridge's with a brass cage containing a parrot that was singing dirty songs,' I pointed out.

'But that's quite different, darling, that's a *bird*. You know all the English are animal lovers.'

'I bet they'd make an exception with Moses,' I said. 'Anyway, go on. What did you get at Fortnum's?'

'Well, they had fruit and nuts, of course, and I bought him a big box of liqueur chocolates, because I knew he'd like them. But, you know, darling, how Fortnum's prides itself on having everything in the *world*?'

'So they say,' I agreed.

'Well, I caught them out. They didn't have the two things that the sailor said Moses particularly liked,' she said.

'And what were those?'

'Well, the sailor said that he always fancied a bit of crumpet and Bristol Cities.'

If I could have got my hands on that jolly Jack tar at that moment, his life would have been in grave danger.

'So?' I said.

'Well, they said that crumpet was not in season. I didn't know crumpets had a season, darling, did you? Although, come to think of it, all those little holes in them must be where they shoot them, poor little things, so they must be like grouse.'

'And the other item?'

'Well, I don't think the man really understood what I meant, because he sent me to the lingerie department.'

'So what happened next?'

'Well, I took a taxi back to the hotel. I asked the taxi man if he knew where I could get crumpet and Bristol Cities and he said the only ones he knew of belonged to his wife and she was very attached to them. I asked where she got them and he said they were inherited. Well, I got to Claridge's and the receptionist said that the manager would like to see me. He's a friend of Daddy's so I thought he wanted to give me some flowers or something. So I said I'd see him in my room in five minutes.'

She paused and gazed at her empty glass. I signalled for a refill.

'Of course, the moment I got out of the lift I knew in a jiffy what the manager wanted to see me about.'

'Moses?'

'Yes. He'd woken up and was singing the most *awful* songs you can imagine and you could hear him right down the hall. Well, I rushed to the room but in my panic I dropped the key, then I bent down to pick it up, all my parcels fell out of the carrier and the bag with the oranges split open and there were oranges all over the floor. At that moment the manager arrived.'

She sipped her fresh martini and looked at me with tear-filled eyes.

'Honestly, darling, I've never been so embarrassed in all my life. There was the manager of Claridge's and me on our hands and knees collecting oranges and inside the room there was Moses bawling out some *disgusting* song about a girl with a bum the size of a b-b-b-bathtub.'

I kept my face grave, but inside I was filled with unholy glee at the mental picture her story presented.

'Well, we got into the room and thank goodness Moses stopped singing. He just eyed the manager for a moment and then called him the offspring of a jig-a-jig girl. Darling, what's a jig-a-jig? I never heard of it. Is it like a tango?'

'Somewhat,' I said. 'It was invented in Port Said to – to – to take sailors' minds off the fact that they were far away from their wives.'

'Oh,' she said, pondering this improbable story. 'Well, anyway, the manager was perfectly *sweet*. He said he didn't mind my having Moses in my room, it was all the swearing and singing. He'd had so many complaints from his other customers, he'd have to ask me to remove the bird. So I brought him to the Dorchester. What else could I do? He sang all the way here and called the taxi driver something I won't repeat. He was very rowdy in the reception hall and so I got them to give me a vodka and tonic and while he was drinking that we covered his cage with napkins and rushed him in here and put him under the table. He's been as good as gold ever since.'

'Darling,' I said. 'I think your idea of giving the Reverend Penge a parrot was a very sweet thought. But don't you think that the sooner the reverend takes delivery of his present the better for all of us?'

'Oh, I *do*,' she said. 'That's what I was doing when you arrived, phoning Pengey – that's what he likes to be called – and I told him we'd bring his present round this afternoon and he was delighted.'

'Well, thank God for that. You didn't tell him what it was, I hope.'

'Oh, no, darling. I want it to be a surprise,' she said.

'It'll certainly be that,' I agreed.

We had a somewhat nervous lunch, since there was a lady two tables away who was possessed of a shrill and penetrating laugh. Every time she was amused and gave vent to this bugle-like bray, both of us jumped under the impression that it was Moses bursting into song. Ursula got hiccoughs and had to ask for a wineglass of vinegar which was, according to her, the only known cure for this malady. When we had finished, we faced the problem of getting Moses and his cage out of the restaurant. Two waiters, overseen by Sebastian, crouched under the table, wrapping napkins around the cage. I fancy one or two of the diners wondered what was happening. Finally they had the cage wrapped in linen. They lifted it up and we started on our way in their wake, looking somewhat like a funeral cortége following a dome-shaped coffin draped in white. All went well until one of the waiters caught his toe on a chair leg, stumbled and two of the napkins slipped and fell to the floor. Moses surveyed the assembled diners with a jaundiced eye.

'You greedy lot of buggers,' he observed in a penetrating voice that made every occupant of the room cease whatever they were doing and fasten their attention on us.

'Greedy bastards,' said Moses, just to show he had not exhausted the second letter of the alphabet.

'Get him out of here – quick,' Sebastian hissed. We all fled pre-cipitately, just as Moses started to sing. In reception, I found a copy of *The Times* someone had left, divided it, crossed it, punched a hole in the middle for the cage's rings, and plastered it over Moses just as he started on the second verse of 'Judy O'Kelly'.

'He seems a bit of a problem as a pet, sir, if you don't mind my remarking,' said Sebastian, smiling.

Moses had fallen silent.

'He's going to a good home,' I said. 'He's going to live with a vicar.'

'I had no idea the Church was getting so liberal-minded,' he said. 'It must be a sign of the times.'

Ursula appeared from the ladies' room, bearing two large carrier bags.

'Thank you for your tolerance and help,' I said to Sebastian.

'Any . . .' he began, and then stopped.

'If you were going to say "any time", don't,' I said. 'Once in a lifetime is enough.' I bundled Ursula and Moses into a taxi and gave the address of the Reverend Penge.

'Darling, that was a scrumptious lunch, thank you so much,' she said, kissing me, 'and thank you for being so good about poor Moses.'

As she spoke she was shuffling about in her carrier bags, examining things.

'What have you got in there?' I asked.

'Oh, just a few goodies for the poor old man,' she said. 'A couple of bottles of Scotch because I know he likes his little noggin and I'm sure he can't afford it. Then there's some food for Moses and his favourite drink, and some reading matter for Pengey, poor old duck.'

She pulled out *The Times*, the *Telegraph*, the latest *Vogue*, a copy of *Punch* and, to my incredulous gaze, a copy of *Playgirl*. 'What,' I asked, 'did you get him *that* for?'

'Well, darling, it's part of my plan for redebilitating him, making him mend his ways. He should start thinking more about the opposite sex and less about his own. So I got him *Vogue* and this, so that he could see what he was missing.'

'Have you looked inside *Playgirl*?' I asked.

'No,' she said. 'It's the usual girlie magazine, isn't it?'

'Take a look,' I said, grimly.

It was perhaps unfortunate that she opened it at the center-fold, which showed a very nude, very virile and very large young man in all his glory.

'Oh, my God,' she said, appalled. 'Oh, *my* God.'

'Yes,' I said. 'Hardly the thing to give old Pengey to redebilitate him, is it?'

'Oh, darling, thank *heavens* you noticed. Of course I can't give it to him. But what am I going to *do* with it?'

'Take it back to Claridge's and give it to the manager,' I suggested.

She did not speak to me for the rest of the journey and she left the offending magazine in the taxi.

The Penge residence – if I may call it that – was one of those splendid old houses like an upended shoebox, with two rooms to a floor. The reverend, we discovered, occupied the two attic rooms and so we toiled up four flights of stairs to get to his abode, Ursula's carrier bags and Moses's cage becoming heavier at every step. Eventually, panting, we stopped outside a door on which, rather pathetically, was pinned a card which said: 'The Reverend Mortimer Penge XXX English lessons given, also Bible lessons (Church of England).'

Ursula knocked and the door was thrown open by the Reverend Penge. He was not what I expected. He looked rather like a French bean that has been deprived of light during its formative years. He bent in the same way and had the same troglodyte greenish-white colouring. He wore large horn-rimmed glasses, a roll-top pullover with purple and white stripes and grey flannel trousers. His white hair was in wild disarray and he held his hands in front of him like a rabbit sitting up, his hands dangling as if both wrists were broken.

'Ursula!' he exclaimed. 'My dear child, how simply divine to see you.'

He kissed her chastely on the cheek.

'This is Gerry,' said Ursula.

'Gerry – what an attractive name and *what* an attractive person,' he said, fluttering his eyelids at me. 'You are a lucky, lucky girl. But do come in. Come into my humble abode.'

His humble abode consisted of two rooms, one divided into a minute kitchen and shower, the other acting as a sitting-cum-bedroom, with two lumpy chairs, a threadbare carpet, a narrow divan bed and under it, to my delight, a huge Victorian chamber-pot, decorated tastefully with garlands of pansies and forget-me-nots. Looking out of the window, I saw the reverend had a nice view over a small park, with plane trees, beds of spring flowers, a pond with ducks on it and benches for reclining on.

One by one, Ursula produced her presents, and with each one the reverend got more and more delighted and tearful with joy.

Finally, Ursula mixed an extra large vodka and tonic, lifted a corner of *The Times* and slipped it into Moses's drinking vessel. She let a few moments pass and then, like a conjuror doing a trick, she whipped off *The Times* and revealed to the reverend's amazed gaze Moses slaking his thirst.

'A parrot!' gasped the reverend. 'Oh, I've always wanted a parrot. Does it talk?'

By way of answer, Moses left off imbibing the heavenly Russian liquid to stare at the Reverend Penge.

'Hello, you old bugger,' said Moses, and then once again set to the task of drinking himself into an alcoholic stupor. The Reverend Penge laughed and laughed and laughed – till he cried.

'Oh, my darling Ursula, you could not have brought me anything better,' he crowed.

'Well,' said Ursula, obviously delighted, 'you said you wanted someone to talk to.'

'You're a saint, my dear, a real saint,' said the reverend. I thought grimly that if he had suffered as I had suffered since meeting Ursula at the station that morning, he might have had second thoughts about her saintliness. We chatted for a while and drank a Scotch (which the reverend insisted on broaching) out of a glass, a cracked cup and a tin mug, then we took our leave.

The next two days were blissful. London in those days was a wonderful city, war-torn though it was. To be there in the spring with an enchanting girlfriend was every young man's dream, but few achieved it. I went back to Bournemouth well satisfied.

Ten days later the phone rang.

'Darling, it's me, Ursula.'

'How are you, sweetheart?' I asked, with no sense of impending doom.

'Oh, I'm fine. But, darling, I want you to do something for me, will you please? It's terribly, terribly important. Do say yes, darling, and then I'll tell you what it is. Promise?'

I should have known Ursula by now.

'Of course,' I said, visualizing some trivial errand.

'Well,' she said slowly, 'd'you remember Moses?'

I went cold all over.

'No,' I shouted into the phone. 'No. I will not be involved with that bloody bird again. No, no, no.'

'There's no need to swear, darling,' she said, 'and in any case, you've promised now, so you must. Let me tell you what's happened. Pengey's in prison.'

'In prison? What for?'

'Well, I'm afraid it's partly Moses's fault,' she said. 'You see, Pengey used to take him out in his cage to that nice little park and sit on a bench. And then Moses would start talking and all the young boys would gather round.'

I groaned.

'And then Pengey would ask one of the boys if he would like to see the parrot do acrobatics, and of course the boy would say yes. So Pengey would say well you must come up to my flat because I can't let him out of the cage here in case he flies away. So the boy would go up to Pengey's flat with him. And you can imagine what happened.'

'Only too vividly.' I said. 'How long did he get?'

'Eighteen months,' said Ursula, 'and, darling, I'm so upset about poor Pengey, but I'm so worried about Moses, poor thing. He's got no one to talk to and love him and give him food and vodka. The landlady says she won't keep him any longer as his language is so foul it embarrasses her husband.'

'What's her husband? A bishop?'

'A docker, I think,' said Ursula, 'but that's not the point. Moses must be rescued and that's where you come in.'

'Now look here . . .' I began.

'Darling, you promised, and if you break your promise I will never speak to you again. I would go myself only I can't as I'm organizing a fete.'

I sighed.

'All right, I'll go,' I said, 'but it's the last time I promise you anything.'

'Darling, I love you to bits. You're the most scrumptious man I know.'

'I'm the most foolish man you know,' I said.

So I went. I had a hectic journey by train with Moses. I'd forgotten his vodka, so he was in full voice, so much so that the guard of the train, a strict Methodist, had the police waiting for me at Bournemouth Central Station. It took a lot of explaining, but I managed to get some vodka from the dining car and while I was arguing with the guard and the police, Moses sucked up this heavenly nectar as fast as I could pour it. I kept wondering how much alcohol it would take to kill a parrot, and hoping that I had bought enough.

A MESSAGE FROM
THE DURRELL WILDLIFE CONSERVATION TRUST

Gerald Durrell's childhood efforts at zoo-keeping, which so bemused his long-suffering family, were the beginning of a lifelong dedication to saving endangered species. What he learned on Corfu from mentors such as Theo inspired his crusade to preserve the rich diversity of animal life on our planet.

This crusade to preserve endangered species did not end with Gerald Durrell's death in 1995. His work goes on through the untiring efforts of Durrell Wildlife Conservation Trust.

Over the years many readers of Gerald Durrell's books have been so motivated by his experiences and vision that they have wanted to continue the story for themselves by supporting the work of his Trust. We hope that you will feel the same way today because through his books and life, Gerald Durrell set us all a challenge. 'Animals are the great voteless and voiceless majority,' he wrote, 'who can only survive with our help'.

Please don't let your interest in conservation end when you turn this page. Write to us now and we'll tell you how you can be part of our crusade to save animals from extinction.

Durrell Wildlife Conservation Trust
Les Augrès Manor
Jersey, Channel Islands, JE3 5BP
UK

Website: www.durrell.org
Email: info@durrell.org

extracts reading groups

competitions books new

discounts extracts

competitions

books

new

events books

extracts

new titles reading groups

interviews

events extracts

discounts

new books events

events new

discounts extracts discounts

www.panmacmillan.com

extracts events reading groups

competitions books extracts new

reading groups

events

reading groups

books

events

books